Tempe
a portrait in color

by

Michel F. Sarda

Introduction
by
Mayor Harry Mitchell

Contributing Photographers

Ken Akers
Ben Arnold
Alan Benoit
Jeff Kida
Jim Richardson

Bridgewood Press
Phoenix, Arizona

Acknowledgments

To Mayor Harry Mitchell, for his personal support.

For their help and assistance during the preparation of this book: Ann Bergin, Don Dotts, Julianna Eriksen, Donna Fleischer, Jane and Richard Neuheisel, Sherry Henry.

For their personal tributes: Kamal Amin, John S. Armstrong, Elden G. Barmore, Dr. Lattie F. Coor, Kay Gammage, David Hanna, James L. Helmers, Warren Iliff, John Junker, Richard G. Neuheisel, Alberto Rios, Bruce Snyder, Karsten Solheim, Conrad J. Storad

To Ken Akers, Ben Arnold, Alan Benoit, Jeff Kida, Jim Richardson, for contributing their superb photographic work.

To Brent DeRaad, director of Public Relations of Fiesta Bowl, to Steve Nielsen and Gary Meyer of the City of Tempe Community Development Department, to Alberto Camasto, Art Director at the ASU Publication Design Center, for their cooperation.

For their support and for their dedication to the Tempe community: Allied-Signal, The Buttes, Chase Bank, Fiesta Inn, Forever Living Products, Impra, Motorola, Radisson Tempe Mission Palms, Saint Luke Hospital, Salt River Project, Southwest Ambulance, UDC Homes, .

To Blair and John Armstrong, for their personal insights and documents regarding Samuel Armstrong. To Edward C. Oetting, head of ASU Archives & Manuscripts, for reviewing information in regard of Arizona State University.
To Richard Bauer, Curator of Photographs and Archives, and Scott Solliday, Curator of History at the Tempe Historical Museum, for their expert cooperation.

For their friendly contribution or appearance: James DeMars, Michelle Dittfach, Tex Earnhardt, Kay Gammage, Ron Gasowski, Brigitte Hallier, Octavia Jones, Mayor Harry Mitchell, Florence Nelson, Alberto Rios, Donnalee Sarda, Jill and Brittnee Schirripa.

To my wife Donnalee, for her continuing trust and encouragement.

Grateful acknowledgment for use of the following quotations:
Page 45: by special authorization of author Alberto Rios.
Pp. 19, 33, 97: Saint-John Perse, Bilingual Edition, Princeton University Press 1977.
Pp. 19, Maynard Dixon; p.21, Vada Carlson; p.23 Sharlot M. Hall; p.30, Marharet E. Schevill; p.31 and 97, Badger Clark; p.32, Thomas E. Gallagher; p.35 Milo Wiltbank;
from *Arizona Anthem*, by Blair Morton Armstrong, The Mnemosyne Press, Scttsdale 1982.

Our sincere gratitude to our friend Blair Morton Armstrong
for her remarkable work of collecting Arizona poetry in her book *Arizona Anthem*,
and to Dean Ross for compiling the history of Tempe in *Tempe, Arizona Crossroads*.

We apologize for credits misinterpreted or omitted unintentionally.

Published by Bridgewood Press, an imprint of Sarda Resources, Inc.
4610 North 40th Street, Phoenix, Arizona 85018-3623

Editor	Donnalee R. Sarda	
Design	Sarda Resources, Inc.	
Translations	French	Sarda Resources, Inc.
	Spanish	Pete Navarrete
	German	Birgit Zimmermann
	Japanese	Japanese Communications Consultants, Inc.

Library of Congress Catalog Card Number 93-71292
ISBN 0-927015-06-4 Regular Edition
ISBN 0-927015-07-2 Special City of Tempe Edition
Printed in Singapore

This book is dedicated to the people of Tempe.

Contents

Introduction

by
Harry E. Mitchell
Mayor of Tempe

Tempe is a community that is proud of its history and looks forward with excitement to its future. Our residents and businesses combine to make the city a vibrant, progressive place to live, work and recreate.

Enjoy your stroll through this book, and, if you are not familiar with our community, please take the time to visit. You will find that both this book and our community are expressions of urban delight.

There's something special about Tempe.

by

Michel F. Sarda

After portraying Phoenix and Scottsdale in recent years, I felt compelled to complete this photographicl essay on the Valley of the Sun with a portrait of Tempe. Why? Because there's definitely something special about Tempe.

Phoenix displays the awesome beauty of a blooming metropolis, with the superb buildings and perspectives that make one proud of a community's achievements. Scottsdale is a unique combination of nature and lifestyle, where the colorful roughness of the Sonoran desert suddenly blends into the green delicacy of a golf course. Tempe, possibly because of the mental energy dispersed by the 50,000 students and faculties of Arizona State University, exudes the highly-original flavor of a frontier town turned into an intellectual power plant.

Surprisingly enough, it's while strolling down Mill Avenue that one perceives the strongest *urban* feeling among all of the places in the Valley – urban being understood here in its original meaning of courteous and welcoming. As a long-time architect and city planner, I know the reason for this feeling: Tempe is built at the right *scale*, respectful of how many building blocks the human mind can encompass, of how far human legs can walk. In this regard, the city has a very European quality, although it could not be more southwestern in many other respects. This paradoxical combination makes for the charm of Tempe.

When my son Bruno was in college at ASU in the late 1980s, he shared an apartment with friends at Hayden Square. Each time I visited him, something deep inside told me that this was a place where I could also live and work, a place where you instantly feel both cozy and energized.

(continued)

Because these impressions remained attached to good memories (my son graduated successfully,) I wanted to dig a little into what suggested them in the first place. Also, being myself some kind of an overschooled intellectual oddity (just ask my wife Donnalee,) I wanted to nose around this fortress of knowledge called ASU, where a mushrooming of innovative buildings had attracted my keen attention for the past ten years. Actually I didn't stop at ASU, I took my notepad and cameras to every spot I thought belonged to an honest description of Tempe.

The resulting portrait that is presented to the reader is exactly that: a portrait. No more, no less: it depicts Tempe and its community at a particular moment in time; it also unveils the relationship between the physical environment of a city and the group of people that belong to it at various levels of interest and dedication. As any creative work, it was also self-revealing for the author: I went through the same process already experienced in preparing previous books, from disappointment (usually a result of unfounded expectations) to gratifying satisfactions. Do I know Tempe better today ? I'm not sure, because this is such a vibrant living organism, incredibly active and ever-changing like life itself, constantly dancing between regeneration and growth. The rehabilitation of Downtown Tempe, the Rio Salado Project, the ongoing freeway system and the improvements of the north bank of the Salt River to name a few, are examples of this seemingly Brownian, feverish activity that shapes the future of the city.

A crossroad of cultures, Tempe offers the best of the West, when open spaces become open minds, when education and hard work translate into an appealing lifestyle, when the magical beauty of nature is complemented by the achievements of a human vision.

The Founding of a City

A Tempe Historical Summary

Hayden Mill, Casa Vieja and Hayden warehouses circa 1887.
(courtesy Tempe Historical Museum)

The Land Legacy

The Salt River valley where Tempe is located was already inhabited in prehistoric times. In the first centuries A D, the Hohokam civilization farmed this land after digging an elaborate network of irrigation canals. Their sudden and mysterious disappearance was probably the consequence of a prolonged drought. Later, Pimas and other sedentary Native American tribes established their homes in the valley and cultivated its soil. These peaceful people never had to face the tragedies of foreign conquests, neither from the Spaniards who preferred the cooler uplands of New Mexico, nor from the American settlers, long discouraged by the harsh climate and the ubiquitous presence of Apache raiders.

Arizona became a territory in 1863 to contribute its mineral resources to the fight of the Union. After the Civil War ended in 1865, the U.S. Army established Fort McDowell at the east end of the valley. This military presence and protection attracted pioneers. In 1867, an adventurer named Jack Swilling came from the mining town of Wickenburg, and planned to rebuild the ancient Hohokam irrigation system to lure farmers to the area. An unstable and violent character (he died ten years later in a Yuma jail,) Swilling is credited for founding Phoenix. Among the new settlers and early associates of Swilling, was Darrell Duppa, an educated and travelled Englishman. When sober, Duppa could display an unusual culture; for the land south of the Salt River, with its towering buttes, he suggested the name of Tempe, after the mythological Vale of Tempe in ancient Greece, home of the lesser gods. The stage was set for the founder of Tempe, Charles Trumbull Hayden, to step in.

The Early Days

In 1866, the U.S. Army's Arizona headquarters were moved from Tucson to Prescott, a disaster for Hayden, a long-time Tucson resident who was in the business of supplying the Army with food and grain. Hayden, born in 1825 in Hartford County, Connecticut, had come to Arizona in 1858. A determined man, he decided to keep serving his military clients by driving his wagons on the five-day uphill journey to Prescott. He was given directions to the best crossing of the Salt River, which he had never crossed before, and found it easily at the foot of what is now the Tempe Butte. The river was flooded and there was no way across. Obliged to camp on the southern bank until the water would subside, Hayden occupied his forced leisure time by climbing to the top of the butte, and there he liked what he saw. Legend has it that Charles Trumbull Hayden, from atop this 300-foot hill, envisioned the new community he would create.

In 1870, after many trips to Prescott, Hayden joined Swilling in digging irrigation canals; the same year, the city of Phoenix was founded and the Hayden Milling and Farming Ditch Company was incorporated. Hayden laid claim to the 160 acres south and west of the butte, where he established his milling business and his living quarters. In 1871, the territorial legislature created Maricopa County and established the county seat in Phoenix.

The newly-built canals helped develop a successful agricultural activity: fruits, citrus, alfalfa, vegetables and cotton. Noah Broadway, B.F. Hardy, James T. Priest — these canal builders are remembered after their names were given to major streets of Tempe.

The untamed Salt River continued to be an obstacle between the different settlements of the Valley of the Sun. Industrious Hayden built and operated a wooden ferry boat, large enough to accommodate a stagecoach.

For a time, the small community on the south bank of the river was called Hayden's Ferry. It was not until 1879 that the name Tempe was officially adopted and recorded by the U.S. Post Office.

Hayden, known as "Don Carlos" by his mostly Hispanic employees, opened a general store. In 1874, his mill was operational; it is still in existence, and is considered today the oldest business in Arizona. Two years later, Hayden married Sallie Davis, a school teacher from California. The couple provided the only social life on this side of the river.

(top)
Hayden's Ferry, c. 1887.

(above)
Charles Trumbull Hayden (right, with beard) in front of the old Hayden house, c. 1879.
(courtesy Tempe Historical Museum)

When Mormon pioneers settled a few miles east, Hayden was so welcoming and helpful, providing them with jobs and basic services at a time when Mormons were persecuted, that his name was first given to the new town before it became known as Mesa, now the second largest city in Arizona. The Mormon influence remains important to both the economy and the political leadership of Tempe, which counts 23 wards (churches) of the Church of Jesus-Christ of the Latter-day Saints.

When Hayden's children reached school age, there was not a single high school in Arizona Territory. The few available teachers, mostly female, were quickly taken away from the classroom by marriage – this was the case for Mrs. Hayden herself. In the fall of 1884, Charles Hayden's concern motivated him into action. An established businessman and a respected citizen, he activated a large network of friends and connections to coach his young business manager,

John Samuel Armstrong, into the Territorial Assembly for the sole purpose of bringing a teacher-training school, called a Normal School, to Tempe. A born politician, Armstrong was not slow to deliver. He maneuvered astutely in the midst of such frenetic lobbying that two grand juries later investigated the misconduct of the Assembly. The Normal School, with an appropriation of $5,000, was signed into law by March, 1885 by Governor Frederick A. Tritle. Few people understood the potential of this modest investment for the future of Tempe.

Hayden wasted no time. Heading the Board of the new school, he raised money within the community, purchased some land, contracted for the building, and hired Hiram Bradford Farmer from New York, to fill all the positions from principal to secretary.

Incorporation and Statehood

The influence of Charles Trumbull Hayden would soon diminish as a consequence of the arrival of new educated settlers, and also due to several personal tragedies: the loss of his daughter Annie, a fire that destroyed most of his business, and financial difficulties that brought him to the verge of bankrupcy. His adamant opposition to the incorporation of Tempe was unsuccessful in 1894, and Dr. Fenn J. Hart was appointed the first mayor of the newborn town. In the following years, telephone and electricity installed. Tempe was no longer a frontier town.

In 1887, the connection of the Southern Pacific Railroad to Tempe, and later to Phoenix, had boosted the economy by permitting fast and easy shipping of cattle and farm produce. A regular influx of new citizens brought entrepreneurial spirit to the young community. Among those who contributed to the betterment of Tempe: Tom and James Goodwin, Charles and Ellen Corbell, Jo Mullen, Isaac Hanna, just to name a few. Soon, Tempe had a newspaper and a bank. However, at the turn-of-the-century, the total population of Tempe was only 900.

The disastrous floods of 1891 and 1905 reminded all dwellers along the banks of the Salt River that nature still had the final say. The construction of the Roosevelt Dam between 1905 and 1911 not only tamed the turbulent river, but changed the future of the Valley of the Sun by providing a seemingly unlimited water supply.

(top) Laird & Dines Drugstore, c. 1900.
(above) Salt River flood of 1905. The wrecked Santa Fe Railroad Bridge had been built only ten years earlier, in 1895.
(courtesy Tempe Historical Museum)

country.

At the same time, President William Howard Taft was supporting Arizona's statehood, which became effective on St. Valentine's Day, February 14, 1912, with George W. P. Hunt as first governor. Carl Hayden, Charles Hayden's son, was elected as the first (and at that time the only) representative of Arizona in the U.S. Congress, where he had one of the longest and most brilliant political careers in the history of this country.

Teddy Roosevelt came to Arizona for the inauguration of what is still today the largest masonry dam in the world. He stopped in Tempe and addressed an enthusiastic crowd from the stairs of Old Main, the second building of the Tempe Normal School and now the oldest one on the campus of Arizona State University.

Teddy Roosevelt addressing a crowd in front of Old Main after the inauguration of the Roosevelt Dam in 1911.
(courtesy Tempe Historical Museum)

Modern Times

Benjamin B. Moeur and his wife Honor arrived from Arkansas in 1896. Moeur, a physician, became a popular figure of Tempe during his four decades of medical practice. In 1932, he ran for governor against the seven-time Governor George Hunt, and won. The famous humorist Will Rogers said of this election: "All those babies he delivered grew up and voted for him." A building at ASU perpetuates the name of Benjamin Moeur.

In 1929, a few weeks before the Wall Street stock market disaster, the Tempe citizens were so confident in their future that they redesigned their town charter and reorganized into the City of Tempe, whose first mayor was druggist Hugh Laird. The same year, the construction of a new bridge was voted. Mill Avenue Bridge was dedicated in 1933 by Governor Moeur and Tempe Mayor Forrest Ostrander.

As World War II came to a close, Tempe counted 5,000 inhabitants, and was not significantly larger than Charles Hayden's initial 320-acre settlement. The G.I. Bill, by sending hundreds of thousands of veterans to college, provided the detonator for Tempe's explosive growth. In just fifteen years, from 1945 to 1960, the population augmented five-fold to 25,000, creating great pressure for the implementation of new urban equipment and services. Today, with more than 150,000 residents, Tempe is the fifth-largest city in Arizona.

Old Main in its semi-rural environment, c. 1920.
(courtesy Tempe Historical Museum)

Arizona State University

In the late 1890s, the Tempe Normal School, embellished with a new superb Main Building (now Old Main,) went through a quiet revolution under the authority of Frederick M. Irish, who introduced programs well suited for the Arizona agricultural environment.

His successor, Arthur J. Matthews, is also credited with significant changes: in 1925 the name of the school became the Tempe State Teachers College, then it changed again in 1929 into the Arizona State Teachers College.

In 1933, Dr. Grady Gammage became president of ASTC. During his 25-year plus presidency, the small provincial school became a university, new buildings sprouted across the campus, enrollment grew ten-fold, and academic and athletic achievements earned national recognition.

At the end of World War II, with Valley of the Sun communities showing the fastest growth in the State, and with the great number of veterans wanting to complete their education, Dr. Gammage defeated the fierce opposition of Tucson's University of Arizona to gain university status, which was fully granted in 1954, under the governorship of Tempean Howard Pyle. The name Arizona State University necessitated still another battle which was won in the general election of 1958. The innumerable achievements of Dr. Gammage earned him the well-deserved title of "Father of ASU." Among the most visible of these accomplishments are the Grady Gammage Memorial Auditorium, initiated with his friend, architect Frank Lloyd Wright, and the Sun Devil Stadium, which grew from 30,000 seats to the grandiose 75,000-seat facility of today.

With 45,000 students and 6,000 faculty, with some of the best research programs in the country and with a campus punctuated with facilities of outstanding architectural quality, Arizona State University is now the fifth largest university in the United States.

(left, opposite page) View of Mill Avenue,
looking north from Fifth Street, c. 1910.
In the background are Papago and Camelback Mountains.
(courtesy Tempe Historical Museum)

Special acknowledgment to Dr. Dean Smith, whose attractive and well-documented history of Tempe in his book *Tempe, Arizona Crossroads* provided most of the information for this summary.

Index of Color Plates

Map of Tempe

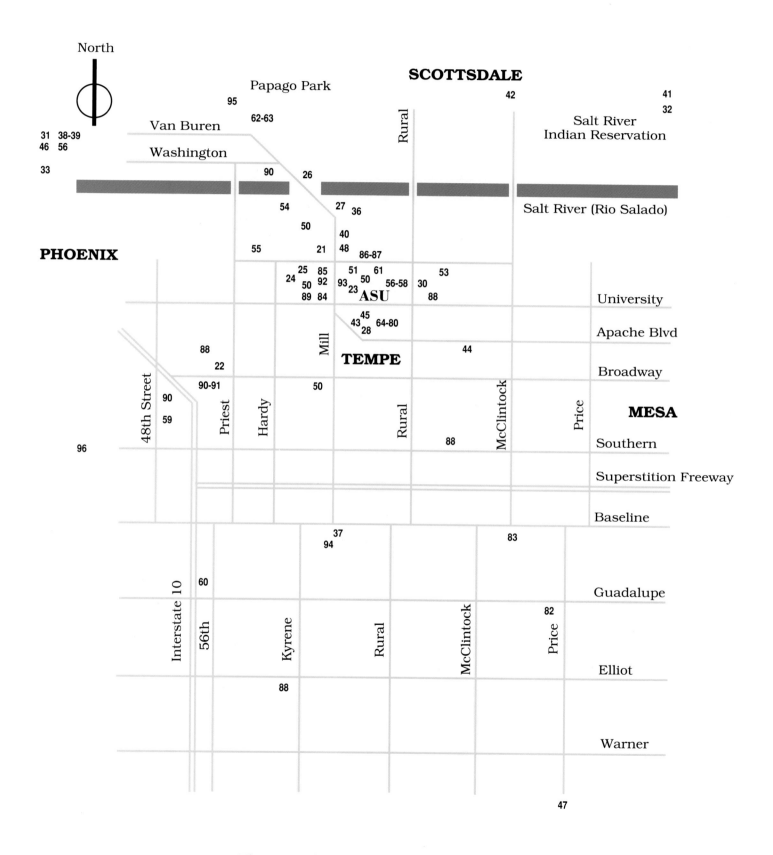

The numbers on the map approximately indicate the locations where the photographs were taken. Each refers to the page on which the photograph appears, as listed page 16.

Legacy

... Out of the dust of dreams
long held and true to my waking
I who hold the black bowl of visions
come with the answer of thunder-topped mesas
and revelation of star-travelled plains.

Maynard Dixon

The horsemen under their morions, grafted to
their mounts, to the creaking of leather, amongst
brambles of another race...
With their beards over their shoulders and their
weapons in profile, from time to time they halted
to measure, on the stone tiers,
the high rising of lands into the sky behind them
to the rising of the waters.

Saint John Perse

(opposite page)
The New Year's Day Fiesta Bowl Parade makes
the characters of the old West come alive.
(photo Michel F. Sarda)

For thousands of years, water brought
prosperity – and trouble – to the inhabitants
of the Salt River Valley. It still glitters like gold
in the sunset.
(photo courtesy of Rio Salado Project)

(opposite page)
The Old Wall is all that remains of the first
home of Charles Trumbull Hayden, founder
of Tempe. Built in 1871, its construction
utilized the mud block masonry technique
called adobe. Carl Hayden, a long time United
States Senator from Arizona and Dean of
Congress was born here. The Old Wall remains
part of Monti's Casa Vieja, a popular
restaurant in downtown Tempe.
(photo Michel F. Sarda)

There's no dissembling in adobe walls;
Dirt they were and dirt they will remain,
Yet in their humble strength
They stand in dignity upon the sunbaked plain,
As though in gratitude
To men whose calloused hands
First formed the ragged bricks
And built of them an earthy sacristy
For treasures held most dear.

Vada Carlson

The Petersen House, built in 1892 by trader
Niels Petersen, is Tempe's most representative
example of late 19th-century Victorian style.
(photo Michel F. Sarda)

These rough walls the memories hold
Of the long-past days of gold;
Through the ever'open doors,
In across the earthen floors,
Came the men who dared to take
Far trails for a new state's sake
Here they councilled, man with man;
Here they reckoned plan by plan
That the present be secure
And the future state endure.

Sharlot M. Hall

An example of the Neo-Colonial Revival Style in favor at the turn of the century, Governor Benjamin B. Moeur's residence was constructed a year after the Petersen's. Recently restored, it is now home to the Tempe Community Council.
(photo Michel F. Sarda)

Tempeans are proud of their history, and carefully preserve their landmarks. The old hardware store on Mill Avenue is today an active theater.

(opposite page)
The Hackett House, built in 1888, the oldest fired red brick building in Tempe, is now home to the Tempe Sister City Corporation, a volunteer organization promoting international good will.

(photos Michel F. Sarda)

Tempe, Arizona, was the first city in America to establish a Sister City relationship with a city in an eastern Europe nation. This special affiliation took place in 1971 when Tempe offered the international hand of friendship to Skopje, Yugoslavia (now Macedonia) – also the birth place of 1979 Peace Nobel Prize Mother Teresa.

This step took courage and long range vision. Tempe went on to form highly successful Sister City programs with Regensburg, Germany; Lower Hutt, New Zealand; Zhennjiang, China; and Timbuktu, Mali in West Africa.

Tempe has received national recognition from the Reader's Digest Foundation for having one of the finest international programs in America. Programs include exchange of students; high school teachers; elementary school teachers; professional and cultural exchanges; an international cooking school called Cuisines of the World; several annual international festivals including the Way Out West Oktoberfest; and operation of Tempe's Hackett House. All of this work is accomplished by volunteers.

Richard G. Neuheisel
President, Sister Cities International

25

Tempe is poised to realize a great, long-held dream. Under a project called Rio Salado, the normally dry Salt River bed and its banks will be converted into the City's most stunning attraction. The central feature will be a two-mile long lake for sailing, boating, fishing, even swimming. Suddenly, Tempe will be a lake-front city.

The Town Lake also will serve as a beautiful backdrop for shoreline development all across Tempe. Shops, restaurants, theaters, office buildings, condos plus parks, trails, and a wide variety of sports facilities, all will be a part of Rio Salado.

Much of the infrastructure – new roads, new bridges, river channelization – is complete or under construction. In a few years the Rio Salado Project is expected to attract millions of visitors a year, create thousands of jobs and provide Tempeans with greatly enhanced opportunities for recreation, entertainment and leisure time enjoyment.

David L. Hanna
Chairman, Tempe's Rio Salado Advisory Commission

(above)
The Mill Avenue Bridge, completed in 1933,
was at that time the largest bridge in Arizona.
(photo courtesy of Rio Salado Project)

(opposite page)
Established by city founder Charles Trumbull
Hayden in 1872, the Hayden flour mill is the
oldest Arizona industry in operation.
(photo Michel F. Sarda)

Among the events at the September, 1964 dedication ceremonies of Grady Gammage Memorial Auditorium, Eugene Ormandy conducted the Philadelphia Philharmonic Orchestra in the hall's first performance. Along with Beethoven's Ninth Symphony, the orchestra appropriately played Richard Strauss's "A Hero's Life." After the applause had died down, Mr. Ormandy returned to the podium and said to a hushed audience: "This is not only the most beautiful room I have ever played in, but acoustically it is the finest I have ever experienced."

Seven years earlier, on a warm May afternoon, Frank Lloyd Wright, ASU President Grady Gammage and Vice President Gilbert Cady walked the length and breadth of the campus, seeking a site for a university auditorium. No ordinary structure, it was to be a cultural and fine arts center as well. Mr. Wright studied the grassy acreage of the women's athletic field in the southwest corner of the campus and, noting its circular frontage, declared: "I believe this is the site. The structure should be circular in design, with outstretching arms saying 'welcome to Arizona'."

In the same year, Mr. Wright traveled to Bagdad to meet with King Faisal II and other Iraqi officials for initial consultations on a cultural center, one of whose main components was an opera house. Preliminary drawings were prepared over the next months. However, due to the overthrow in 1958 of the Iraqi government and the assassination of the king, the project was abandoned. It was disarmingly sensible to transpose the Bagdad opera house to another desert environment – the Sonoran desert in Arizona.

Neither Mr. Wright nor Dr. Gammage lived to see their dream materialize. Mr. Wright died on April 9, 1959 and Dr. Gammage died December 22nd of the same year. With the staunch support of regents and civic leaders such as Walter Bimson, O.D. Miller, Lewis Ruskin and Lynn Laney, the project remained on track. The Arizona legislature voted funds for the structure in its 1961 session and the Board of Regents approved President Homer Durham's recommendation that the building be named, "The Grady Gammage Memorial Auditorium." On May 23rd, 1962, 11-year-old Grady Gammage Jr. turned the first shovel of earth at the official ground breaking ceremony. Construction was in progress for 25 months and was completed well before the formal dedicatory events of September, 1964.

Kamal Amin
Architect and Structural Engineer
Former member of the Frank Lloyd Wright design team
for the Grady Gammage Memorial Auditorium

The Grady Gammage Memorial Auditorium,
on the campus of Arizona State University, is
Tempe's utmost landmark.
(photo Alan Benoit)

In beauty the old men will regard you.
In beauty the old women will regard you.
In beauty the young men will regard you.
In beauty the young women will regard you.
In beauty the boys will regard you.
In beauty the girls will regard you.
In beauty the children will regard you.
Happily as they all go to their homes
They will regard you.
May their roads home
Be on the peaceful trail.

Navajo Prayer
transcribed by Margaret Erwin Schevill

Every year at Arizona State University, the
Pow Wow complements the more traditional
graduation ceremonies by honoring with pride
the graduating Native American students.
(photo Michel F. Sarda)

... Give me work that's open to the sky;
Make me a pardner of the wind and sun,
And I won't ask a life that's soft or high.

Badger Clark

The merry crew of this stagecoach participates
in the annual Fiesta Bowl Parade.
(photo Michel F. Sarda)

Then,
All my mysteries
I will unfold
And you shall see
Into eternity...

Thomas E. Gallagher

The Sonoran desert surrounds the Salt River
valley where Tempe is situated. With its
beautiful sceneries and distinctive giant
saguaros, it is more a garden than a hostile
wilderness.

(photo Michel F. Sarda)

These were very great forces at work on the causeway of men –
very great forces of labour
Holding us outside of custom and holding us outside of season,
among men of custom, among men of season,
And on the savage stone of misfortune restoring to us the land,
by vintage bared, for new nuptials.

Saint John Perse

Adjacent Phoenix seems to rise from embers
– deserving its mythological name – in a fiery
Arizona sunset.

(photo Michel F. Sarda)

The presence in Tempe of Arizona State
University, one of the largest universities in
the United States, attracts young educated
people from all over the world. Forty-five
nationalities are represented at ASU.
(photo Michel F. Sarda)

People

I'd like to live in the kind of town
That's building up, not tumbling down.
A hustling, bustling, busy place
Where there's always things to do.
A town that's run for the good of all,
And not for just a few.

Milo Wiltbank

The Tempe Butte is a distinctive landmark and a playground for children and adults. The huge letter once was an N for Normal School, then a T for Tempe State Teachers College. Today, the A stands for Arizona State University.

(photo Michel F. Sarda)

New "settlers" are not long before enjoying and supporting their community of adoption. This group heralds the colors of the Phoenix Suns, who competed for the National Basketball Association Championship in June, 1993.

(photo Michel F. Sarda)

Every year, the Fiesta Bowl Parade offers an
opportunity to revive traditions. A little girl
displays southern romantic elegance.
(photo Michel F. Sarda)

A young Hopi dancer is absorbed in his memories.

(photo Michel F. Sarda)

Fiesta Bowl races are among many events
that bring the community and visitors
together.
(photo Ken Akers, courtesy of Fiesta Bowl)

Floating down the Verde River is a summer
experience young people wouldn't miss.
(photo Alan Benoit)

Florence Nelson founded the Desert Discovery
Center to introduce Arizona residents and
visitors to the fragile splendors – and to the
tenants – of the Sonoran desert. The Center,
working in coordination with other
environmental programs of Arizona State
University, also provides archeological
presentations on the ancient human
inhabitants, the Hohokams.

(photo Michel F. Sarda)

"When my husband Grady saw the finished plans for the grand auditorium he said: "You see, it does say 'Welcome to all the world,' just as Mr. Wright envisioned."
Mrs. Grady Gammage

Kay Gammage happily shares memories of her late husband, former ASU president Grady Gammage, dealing with Frank Lloyd Wright. They both initiated what is now the Gammage Auditorium – one of the finest concert halls in the world.

(photo Michel F. Sarda)

Ron Gasowski, a professor of art at ASU and
a successful artist, unleashes his imagination
in creating poetic sculptures by using found
and hand-made ceramic objects.
(photo Michel F. Sarda)

In light something is lifted.
That is the property of light,
And in it one weighs less.

Light, the slow moment of everything fast:
Like hills, those slowest waves, light
That slowest fire, all
Confusion, confusion here
One more part
Of clarity.

Alberto Rios

James DeMars (right), a professor at the ASU School of Music, is receiving nationwide attention for his compositions blending classical and native American instruments, and for a new work entitled *An American Requiem.* Poet Alberto "Tito" Rios (left), head of the ASU English Creative Writing Programs, has received national recognition for his work. Together they produced a cantata based on Rios' poems entitled *Tito's Say.*

(photo Michel F. Sarda)

The Tempe Diablos are a group of civic leaders sincerely committed to the betterment and welfare of Tempe. Each year, they raise over $250,000 to support charitable organizations that benefit youth, education, and recreation in our community.

The Diablos are the official hosts for the Fiesta Bowl, extending our hospitality to the thousands of fans that come to Tempe for the annual New Year's Day event.

James L. "Jamey" Helmers
Tempe Diablos

Tempe Mayor Harry Mitchell enjoys the company of Miss Arizona in the Fiesta Bowl Parade, along with Tempe Diablos' dedicated volunteers.

(photo Alan Benoit)

Tex Earnhardt started one of the most successful car dealerships in America when Tempe was agricultural land. A long-time participant in rodeos, he rides here the Brahma bull that has become his trademark.
(photo Michel F. Sarda)

The Phoenix Cardinals are the Valley of the Sun's National Football League franchise team. Their headquarters are located in Tempe. Fans harbor their colors with pride.
(photo Michel F. Sarda)

Community

When I was growing up, Tempe was considered a little stodgy – not as progressive as its neighboring cities. But look at us now! We're a city in the forefront, with high-tech industry, tourism, professional sports, and thriving business to go along with our great university. We are very proud and very optimistic about our future.

Harry Mitchell, mayor of Tempe

Art and creativity are omnipresent ingredients of the cityscape. From top left, clockwise: bronze Jackrabbits by sculptor Mark Rossi at CenterPoint; "Who let the swan out of the garage?" by sculptor Bobby Joe Scribner; the new Tempe library; entrance to the Performing Arts Center.

(photos Michel F. Sarda)

The elegant reversed pyramid of Tempe City
Hall, an unusual although logical energy-
efficient solution to provide internal spaces
with shade, is an unmistakable feature in
downtown Tempe.

(photo Michel F. Sarda)

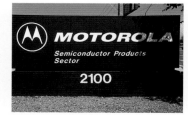

International corporations and major local businesses are attracted to Tempe because of its convenient location adjacent to Phoenix and a major airport, by the large research resources provided by Arizona State University, and by an alluring lifestyle.
(photos Michel F. Sarda)

With merely a wasteland of acreage to work with, a group of dedicated men and women pooled their resources to transform part of Tempe's Salt River bed into the acclaimed Karsten Golf Course at Arizona State University. Under the direction of noted golf architect Pete Dye, an actual junkyard was magically converted into a picturesque championship golf course.

The scenic public links, host of the 1992 NCAA Women's Championship and the annual site of the PING Phoenix Junior Championship, provides a facility to make the citizens of Tempe and the ASU Sun Devil men's and women's golf teams proud.

"We wanted the college students to have a place to play golf and to be able to call it their home. It should leave memories for them the rest of their lives."

Karsten Solheim
Karsten Manufacturing Corporation

Arizona Public Service's space-station-like power plant is a high-tech backdrop to the inviting greenery of the Karsten Golf Course.
(photo Michel F. Sarda)

Amtrak keeps alive Tempe's oldest tradition as a crossroad. Visible in the background is the white pyramid-shaped tomb of George Hunt, Arizona's first governor.
(photo Michel F. Sarda)

Phoenix's Sky Harbor International is one of the busiest airports. Visions of airplanes landing and taking off are part of the Tempe skyscape.

(photo Michel F. Sarda)

At the turn of every New Year, the Fiesta Bowl
parade, marching band contest and football
game become the center of national attention.
(Left: photos Ben Arnold, Jeff Kida, courtesy of
Fiesta Bowl. Right: photos Michel F. Sarda)

Following the initial Fiesta Bowl game in 1971, Arizona Governor Jack Williams looked into his crystal ball and stated: "We have every confidence that the caliber of this great sports event will be heightened even more in the years to come."

To think that over 20 years later, the Fiesta Bowl has grown to be one of America's top bowl games; to think that the Fiesta Bowl festival consisted of 10 events in 1971 and now stages 60 year-round events; to think that the Fiesta Bowl Parade is Arizona's largest one-day spectator event, attracting over 300,000 street spectators; one has to wonder if Williams ever imagined this much success.

It was all merely an idea in 1968, when former ASU president G. Homer Durham mentioned the plan at an awards banquet. But with the hard work and determination of thousands of Arizona volunteers, the Fiesta Bowl has climbed to the top, and continues to follow its initial guiding principle: the Fiesta Bowl will develop a multi-event festival that will revolve around one of the nation's top collegiate bowl games.

John Junker
Fiesta Bowl Executive Director

An aerial view reveals the impressive architecture of ASU's Sun Devil Stadium, which accommodates 75,000 people.
(photo Jeff Kida, courtesy of Fiesta Bowl)

Arizona State University football is an institution in Tempe and the Valley of the Sun. It is the oldest sports entity in the Valley and thousands of alumni and fans support the program.

ASU is nationally known for its gridiron success. Names like Danny White, David Fulcher, John Jefferson, Mike Haynes, Charley Taylor, Woody Green, Al Harris and J.D. Hill roll off the tongue of sports fans everywhere. To date, almost 12 million fans have watched the Sun Devils play football in Sun Devil Stadium alone.

Bruce Snyder
Head Football Coach, Arizona State University

The ASU football team, the Sun Devils, plays at home in front of enthusiastic crowds.
(photo Jim Richardson, courtesy of ASU)

The sunny weather of Arizona is a blessing
for baseball teams training in the spring. The
California Angels have adopted the new Tempe
Diablo Stadium.
(photo Michel F. Sarda)

The small adjacent community of Guadalupe, established by Yaqui immigrants from Mexico earlier this century, proudly displays its cultural identity on outdoor murals.
(photo Michel F. Sarda)

The Islamic Center's mosque in downtown
Tempe gracefully illustrates the diversity of
cultures that makes this community special.
(photo Michel F. Sarda)

(above and opposite page)
Surrounded by ponds and luxuriant vegetation, the Phoenix Zoo is the largest, non-tax supported zoo in the world. Located partially in Tempe in Papago Park, just across the Salt River, it provides pleasant wanderings to nature and animal lovers. Clockwise from top left: Ducks at their games; a black-tail jackrabbit; a family of *javelinas* at rest; a dove nested in a saguaro cactus.
(photos Michel F. Sarda)

The Phoenix Zoo was opened in 1962 and specializes in Arizona Trail animals along with two major exhibit areas on Africa and the tropics. At the latter, a new Tropical Flights exhibit was opened that features tropical plantings and primarily endangered forest birds and bats from across the world.

One of the zoo's primary emphasis is conservation and they are proud of having helped save the severely endangered Arabian oryx. In 30 years, the Zoo has propagated over 250 oryx and in that time the world's oryx population has risen from less than 50 to over 1000! The Zoo also features such endangered species as the Sumatran tiger, orangutan, Galapagos tortoise, Grevy's zebra, sand cats, cheetah and Bali mynas.

The Zoo also concentrates on education programs and currently has two children's zoos to provide interactive learning programs for young students. There is also an experimental Insect Lab and touch-carts in the Arizona Trail where volunteers provide learning opportunities for adults and families.

Warren Iliff, Phoenix Zoo Executive Director

Works of contemporary art transform the campus of Arizona State University into a intriguing outdoor art gallery. Jerry Peart's *Celebration* was commissioned in 1984 for the ASU Centennial festivities.
(photo Michel F. Sarda)

Arizona State University

Arizona State University celebrates the rugged heritage, the distinctive character and the dynamic spirit it shares with its hometown and partner, the City of Tempe. Both the University and the City are products of the vision of Arizona pioneer Charles Trumbull Hayden and tough-minded citizens such as John S. Armstrong and Martha Wilson who formed this community while Arizona was still a Territory. For more than a century we have grown and matured together, mutually strengthened by our deeply-established roots.

Today, Arizona State University's Main Campus takes special pride in its home town community situated at the hub of a vigorous, richly-diverse, metropolitan area. It is forward-looking, it is agile, and it is burgeoning with opportunity and promise.

With us it is more than partnership. It is kinship.

Lattie F. Coor
President, Arizona State University

John Samuel Armstrong at age 23 arrived in Arizona in 1879 with his bride Sarah. He had received a federal appointment as teacher to the Pima Indian Reservation. For three years, he taught with his wife in Sacaton. Moving to Tempe he first became Charles Trumbull Hayden's business manager, then for a time, partner with Niels Petersen in a mercantile business which he bought out forming his own mercantile company. He served as Postmaster and later founded and became the first president of the Bank of Tempe.

In 1884 he was elected to the Territorial Legislature, where he was named chairman of the Education Committee. With utmost skill and tenacity causing him to be hailed as a "political magician" by the newspapers, he legislated Arizona's first institution of higher learning into being, and earned for himself for all time his recognition as Father of Arizona State University.

John S. Armstrong,
grandson of John Samuel Armstrong

ASU Law School's Armstrong Hall is named after the young Territorial Legislator who established in 1885 the Tempe Normal School that later became Arizona State University. Today, the campus also serves as an arboretum displaying a variety of desert-specific and rare vegetal species.
(photo Michel F. Sarda)

A popular passage, Palm Walk crosses the campus from north to south, under the distinctive shade of towering palm trees.
(photo Michel F. Sarda)

ASU's rapid growth in the past two decades has triggered a need for new facilities. Under the supervision of the College of Architecture and Environmental Design, outstanding buildings have been erected that make the ASU campus an attraction in itself for architects. Clockwise from upper left: Activity Center; Student Recreation Center; School of Music; Hayden Library.

(photos Michel F. Sarda)

A group of students enjoy the morning sun of
a cool spring day by the fountain located in
front of the new Life Sciences Building. In the
background stands Old Main, the first
building, erected in 1898, on the campus.
(photo Michel F. Sarda)

The architecture of the new Student Services
Building provides spectacular perspectives.
(photo Jim Richardson, courtesy Arizona State University)

Arizona State University boasts a diverse, talented faculty and a variety of nationally recognized research centers. ASU is a bastion of world-class scholarship, with rich veins of potential technology to be tapped.

A university's primary business is knowledge. As teachers, ASU faculty members introduce students to the fruits of scholarship accumulated over generations. As researchers, they work in the laboratory, library, or at locations in the field using the tools and techniques of scholarship to create new knowledge.

Once created, this new information is transferred to the community in the form of science and technology, as programs designed to deal with various social problems, through the creative works of artists and performers, or via the know-how and skills embedded within graduating students themselves.

But success ultimately depends on a team effort. As a result, research parks and university-affiliated research institutes have become essential junctions in the process of technology and knowledge transfer. Arizona State University has it all.

Conrad J. Storad
ASU Research Publications

This specially-built acoustic chamber illustrates ASU's dedication to cutting-edge scientific research.
(photo Jim Richardson, courtesy Arizona State University)

(above)
Water features are omnipresent on the ASU
campus. They are welcomed by students
during hot summer days.
(opposite page)
The Nelson Fine Arts Center was designed by
noted architect Antoine Predock. It shelters
ASU art collections and offers innovative
indoors-outdoors performing arts spaces.
(photos Michel F. Sarda)

College of Law Library
Expansion and Renovation

Architect:
Leo A. Daly, Phoenix, AZ
In Association with
Scogin, Elam & Bray
Architects, Inc. Atlanta, GA

Construction Manager:
CMX Group, Inc.

General Contractor:
Okland Construction Co., Inc.
Phoenix, Arizona

Completion Date: July 1993

Every year brings a spectacular addition to
the campus skyline. With its futuristic shapes,
the new Law Library perpetuates a tradition
of daring innovation.
(photo Michel F. Sarda)

Arizona State University is now the fifth
largest university in the United States.
Campus walkways and buildings are filled
with scurrying crowds.
(photo Michel F. Sarda)

A reflection of campus life, billboards display
the students' imaginative announcements.
(photo Michel F. Sarda)

ASU campus, which accommodates 45,000
plus students is a small town in itself. The
new wing of the College of Architecture and
Environmental Design contributes to this
urban feeling.

(photo Michel F. Sarda)

The graduation ceremony, here held at the
ASU Activity Center, perpetuates with flying
colors the centuries-old tradition of honoring
the effort involved in acquiring knowledge.
(photo Jim Richardson, courtesy Arizona State University)

The Grady Gammage Memorial Auditorium
provides a spectacular backdrop to the ASU
faculty in full regalia on Graduation Day.
(photo Jim Richardson, courtesy Arizona State University)

From centuries-old irrigation canals to innumerable contemporary fountains, the theme of running and bubbling water is present everywhere in Tempe and on the ASU campus.

(photo Jim Richardson, courtesy of ASU)

Lifestyle

A century ago, Darrel Duppa named Tempe after the enchanting valley of northern Greece where ancient mythology gods had their homes. Today, a vibrant combination of campus town, business center, high-tech and research park, transportation and communication hub in a superb natural setting, Tempe offers a variety of lifestyles to match the most demanding expectations.

In a 1992 survey, Tempe was recognized as the most desirable place to live in the Valley of the Sun.

The miraculous encounter of an ever-blue
sky, abundant water and fertile soil makes
for garden-like residential neighborhoods.
(photo Michel F. Sarda)

Tempe features many lakes for the enjoyment
of its residents.
(photo Michel F. Sarda)

CenterPoint on Mill Avenue is a meeting place of choice for ASU students, faculty and visitors alike. The Tempe Butte is visible in the background.

(photo Michel F. Sarda)

Downtown Tempe was entirely rehabilitated in the past ten years. Hayden Square combines attractive urban housing with offices, shops, restaurants and ongoing entertainment. Tempeans love it.

(photo Michel F. Sarda)

Twice a year, the Tempe Arts Festival, the
largest of its kind in Arizona, brings together
hundreds of artists and intrigued crowds.
(photo Michel F. Sarda)

A face painting artist displays her talent
during the Arts Festival.
(photo Michel F. Sarda)

We consider Tempe a great community to live and to do business in.

Elden G. Barmore
Rio Salado Bank

In recent years, Tempe has emerged as a major business center. Attractive workplaces have mushroomed all across town. Clockwise from top left: ASU Research Center; Fountainhead Corporate Park; University Center; Tempe City Center.
(photos Michel F. Sarda)

A towering addition to the remodeling of
downtown Tempe, the Chase building is the
center of a multi-use project that also includes
the largest movie theater complex in the
Valley.

(photo Michel F. Sarda)

Tempe contributes first-class facilities to the attraction of conventions and tourists to the area. Clockwise from top left: The Buttes, a spectacular Westcourt resort; Red River Opry, a country music theatre; Fiesta Inn's inviting pool; Charley Brown, a romantic restaurant by the lakes.
(photos Michel F. Sarda)

With more than 50 competition golf courses, the Valley of the Sun has established itself as a golfer's heaven. The buttes serve as a backdrop to the practice course at Fiesta Inn.
(photo Michel F. Sarda)

Old Tempe provides entertaining surprises
day after day. The shops at Mill's Court are an
all-time favorite.

(photo Michel F. Sarda)

Mill Avenue combines the charm of a frontier
town with the sophistication generated by
the presence of a large university.
(photo Michel F. Sarda)

In Kiwanis Park, the young generation shows the way to the future with a graceful determination.

(photo Michel F. Sarda)

The flower of the Prickly Pear cactus
symbolizes here the blooming of Tempe out of
the ruggedness of the Sonoran desert.
(photo Michel F. Sarda)

95

Men of the older, gentler soil,
Loving the things that their fathers wrought –
Worn old fields of their fathers' toil,
Scarred old hills where their fathers fought –
Loving their land for each ancient trace,
Like a mother dear for her wrinkled face,
Such as they never can understand
The way we have loved you, young, young land!

Badger Clark

... Men again have found, in the wind,
this way of living and climbing.
Men of fortune, bringing with them,
into new country,
eyes as fertile as rivers.

Saint John Perse

(opposite page)
This view of Tempe illustrates Charles Trumbull Hayden's vision of a vibrant and prosperous community on the southern bank of the Salt River.
(photo courtesy of Rio Salado Project)

97

Appendices

Translations

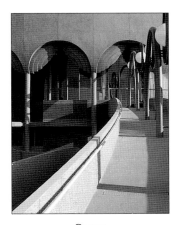

Cover

pages 18-19

Chaque année, la parade du Fiesta Bowl fait revivre les personnages du Far-West légendaire.

El desfile del Fiesta Bowl cada año nuevo hace renacer los personajes del Viejo Oeste.

Die Fiesta Bowl Parade am Neujahrstag läßt die Charaktere des alten Westens wieder aufleben.

元旦の日に開催されるフィエスタ・ボールでは古き良き時代の西部が蘇る。

page 20

Depuis des millénaires, la Rivière Salée apporte aux riverains de sa vallée une prospérité ponctuée d'inondations catastrophiques. Elle a toujours la couleur de l'or dans la lumière du soir.

Por miles de años, el agua ha traído prosperidad – y daño, a los habitantes del Valle de Río Salado. Todavía relumbra como oro en el desierto.

Seit Tausenden von Jahren brachte das Wasser Wohlstand - und Schwierigkeiten - für die Einwohner des Salt River Tales. Es glänzt immer noch wie Gold in der untergehenden Sonne.

何千年もの間ソルト・リバー渓谷に住む住民に潤いを与え、また脅かしてきた流れは今でも夕刻になるとその表面を紺碧に染める。

page 21

Le Vieux Mur est tout ce qui reste de la première demeure de Charles Trumbull Hayden, le fondateur de Tempe. Construite en 1871, cette maison a faite de blocs de boue séchée, une technique nommée adobe. Carl Hayden, qui fut longtemps Sénateur de l'Arizona et Doyen du Congrès, y est né. Ce mur fait aujourd'hui partie de la Casa Vieja de Monti, un restaurant apprécié dans le vieux Tempe.

La Pared Vieja es todo lo que queda de la primera casa de Charles Trumbull Hayden, fundador de Tempe. Construída en 1871, su construcción fue de adobes. Carl Hayden, senador estadounidense por mucho años y décano del congreso, nació aquí. La Pared Vieja permanece parte de la Casa Vieja de Monti, un restaurante muy popular en el centro de Tempe.

Die 'Old Wall' ist alles, was noch von dem ersten Haus von Charles Trumbull Hayden, dem Gründer von Tempe, übriggeblieben ist. Erbaut im Jahr 1871, wurde beim Bau die Maurertechnik mit Schlammblöcken, Adobe genannt, verwendet. Carl Hayden ein langjähriger US Senator aus Arizona und Dean des Congresses wurde hier geboren. die 'Old Wall' ist Teil von Montis Casa Vieja, einem beliebten Restaurant in der Innenstadt von Tempe.

テンピ市の創設者であるチャールズ・トランブル・ヘイデンの最初の家屋は1871年に建設され、現在では古い壁が残るだけとなっている。この建物にはアドビと呼ばれる泥で作られた煉瓦が使われている。アリゾナ州の合衆国上院議員またコングレスの議会長であったカール・ヘイデンはこの家で生まれた。この古い壁はテンピ市のダウンタウンにあるポピュラーなレストラン、モンティース・カサ・ビエハの一部として残っている。

page 22

La maison construite en 1892 par le négociant Niels Petersen est à Tempe l'exemple le plus représen-tatif du style Victorien.

La Casa Petersen, construída en 1892 por el comerciante Niels Petersen, es el ejemplo más representativo del estilo victoriano del siglo 19.

Das Petersen Haus, erbaut im Jahr 1892 vom Händler Niels Petersen, ist das repräsentativste Beispiel des viktorianischen Stils des späten 19. Jahrhunderts.

ピーターセン・ハウスは1892年に商人ニールズ・ピーターセンによって建設されたテンピを代表する19世紀後半のビクトリア調の建造物である。

page 23

Exemple du style néo-colonial en faveur au tournant du siècle, la résidence du gouverneur Benjamin Moeur fut commencée un an après celle de Petersen. Récemment restaurée, elle est aujourd'hui le siège du Conseil Communautaire de Tempe.

Un ejemplo del estilo Revivido Neo-Colonial muy popular al fin del siglo 19, la residencia del Governador Benjamin B. Moeur fue construída después de la Casa Petersen. Reconstruída recientemente, ahora es la casa del Concilio de la Comunidad de Tempe.

Ein Beispiel des neo-kolonial-istischen Stils der zur Jahr-hundertwende beliebt war, ist das Haus von Gouverneur Benjamin B. Moeur, erbaut ein Jahr nach dem Haus der Petersens. Vor kurzem renoviert, beherbergt es jetzt den Stadtrat von Tempe.

20世紀初頭の新植民地が復興したスタイルの良い例が旧知事ベンジャミン B. ムーアの自宅で、ピーターセンの家が作られた一年後に建設されている。この建物は最近修復され、現在ではテンピ・コミュニティー・カウンシルの新事務所として利用されている。

page 24

Les Tempéens sont fiers de leur histoire et en protègent les traces. Un ancien magasin d'outillage sur Mill Avenue a été transformé en théatre.

Los tempineños tienen orgullo de su pasado y conservan sus sucesos. Esta ferretería en la Avenida Mill es actualmente un teatro.

Die Einwohner von Tempe sind stolz auf ihre Geschichte und erhalten mit Liebe ihre Sehenswürdigkeiten. Der alte Eisenwarenladen auf Mill Avenue ist heute ein geschäftiges Theater.

テンピ市民はこの町の歴史を誇りとしており、文化財を丁寧に保存している。ミル・アベニューにある昔の金物店は今日ではアクティブな劇場となっている。

page 25

La Hackett House, de 1888, est la plus ancienne construction de brique de Tempe. Elle sert aujourd'hui de siège à la Tempe Sister City Corporation, une organisation bénévole pour la promotion des relations inter-nationales.

La Casa Hackett, construída en 1888 y la casa más vieja de ladrillo rojo, es ahora la casa de la Corporacíon Tempe Sister City, una organización de voluntarios que promueve la buena voluntad internacional.

Das Hackett Haus, erbaut im Jahr 1888 und das älteste Gebäude in Tempe aus gebrannten roten Ziegeln, beherbergt jetzt die Tempe Sister City Corporation, einem Freiwilligenverband zur Förderung von internationaler Verständigung.

1888年に建設されたハケット・ハウスはテンピで最古の真っ赤な煉瓦でできた建物で、現在では国際親善を促進するボランティアーの組織である、テンピ姉妹都市コーポレーションの事務所として利用されている

page 26

Le pont de Mill Avenue était le plus grand pont d'Arizona lorsqu'il fut terminé en 1933.

El Puente de la Avenida Mill, terminado en 1933, era entonces, el más largo de Arizona.

Die Mill Avenue Brücke, fertiggestellt im Jahr 1933, war zu der Zeit die größte Brücke in Arizona.

ミル・アベニュー橋は1933年に完成し、当時としてはアリゾナで最大規模の橋であった。

page 27

La minoterie Hayden, créée en 1872 par le fondateur de Tempe, Charles Trumbull Hayden, est la plus ancienne industrie d'Arizona en activité.

Establacida por el fundador Charles Trumbull Hayden en 1872, este molino Hayden es la industria más vieja en operación en el estado.

Die Hayden Mühle, errichtet von Stadtgründer Charles Trumbull Hayden im Jahr 1872, ist die älteste Industrieanlage, die noch in Betrieb ist.

1872年に市の創始者であるチャールズ・トランブル・ヘイデンにより設立されたヘイデン・フラワー・ミルはアリゾナで最古の産業を営む施設となった。

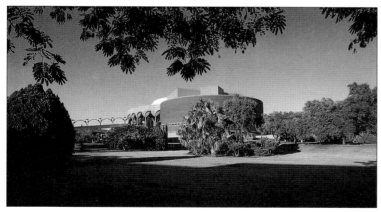

pages 28-29

L'auditorium dédié à la mémoire de Grady Gammage, sur le campus de l'Université d'Etat d'Arizona (ASU), est le monument le plus célèbre de Tempe.

El Auditorio Memorial Grady Gammage, en los terrenos de la Universidad Estatal de Arizona, es el éxito sobresaliente de Tempe.

Das Grady Gammage Memorial Auditorium auf dem Campus der Arizona State University ist Tempes herausragendstes Wahrzeichen.

アリゾナ州立大学のキャンパスにあるグラディー・ガメッジ大講堂はテンピで最も顕著な建物である。

page 30

Chaque année à l'Université, le Pow Wow, réunion indienne rituelle, honore avec fierté les étudiants indiens qui vont être diplômés.

Cado año en los terrenos de la Universidad Estatal de Arizona, el Pow Wow completa las ceremonias más tradicionales de graduación al honorar con orgullo a sus estudiantes indios americanos que gradúan.

Jedes Jahr vervollständigt das Pow Wow an der Arizona State University das mehr traditionell ausgerichtete Zeremoniell der Graduation, indem es mit Würde die Studenten indianischer Abstammung ehrt.

アリゾナ州立大学では毎年ネイティブ・アメリカンの卒業生を誇りを持って表彰している。パウ・ワウのお祭りが伝統的な卒業式に彩りを添えている。

page 31

Le jovial équipage de cette diligence participe à la parade annuelle du Fiesta Bowl.

El equipo alegre de este carruaje participa en el desfile anual del Fiesta Bowl.

Die fröhliche Mannschaft dieser Postkutsche nimmt an der jährlichen Fiesta Bowl Parade teil.

駅馬車上の楽しそうな人達は毎年開催されるフィエスタ・ボール・パレードの参加者である。

page 32

Le désert de Sonora cerne la vallée de la Rivière Salée où Tempe est située. Mais avec ses perspectives superbes et ses cactus géants, les saguaros, cette nature-là ressemble davantage à un parc qu'à un désert hostile.

El desierto Sonorense rodea el Valle del Río Salado donde Tempe está situado. Con sus paisajes bonitos y sus distinguidos saguaros gigantes, es más bien un jardín que un llano hostil.

Die Sonora Wüste umgibt das Tal des Salt River in dem Tempe liegt. Mit seiner herrlichen Szenerie und herausragenden riesigen Saguaros ist es mehr ein Garten als eine feindliche Wildnis.

テンピの町が在るソルト・リバー周辺はソノラン砂漠である。素晴らしい景色と趣の異なった大柱サボテンの背景は厳しい野生の砂漠と言うよりも、ガーデンと言ったほうが的を得ているかもしれない。

page 33

La ville de Phoenix, contigüe à Tempe, semble surgir des braises d'un coucher de soleil, méritant par là son nom mythologique.

Phoenix adjacente parece salir del rescoldo – mereciendo su nombre mitológico, en una puesta de sol arizonense.

Das benachbarte Phoenix scheint aus glühender Kohle - entsprechend seinem mythologischen Namen - von einem feurigen Sonnenuntergang emporzusteigen.

フェニックスはその伝説の名が示すとおり自らの灰の中から蘇った。情熱的なアリゾナのサンセットを象徴しているかのようである。

page 34

La présence à Tempe d'une des plus importantes universités d'Amérique attire des étudiants du monde entier. Quarante-cinq nationalités sont représentées à ASU.

La presencia en Tempe de la U.E. de A. una de las universidades más grandes de los Estados Unidos, atrae a gente joven educada de todo el mundo. Cuarenta y cinco nacionalidades son representadas.

Die Gegenwart der Arizona State University in Tempe, einer der größten Universitäten in den USA, lockt junge Menschen aus der ganzen Welt. 45 Nationalitäten sind an der ASU vertreten.

テンピ市のアリゾナ州立大学は全米でも最大規模であり、世界中から若い教育された人々を集めている。45ヶ国の人々がアリゾナ州立大学で学んでいる。

page 36

La Butte de Tempe est une curiosité locale et un lieu récréatif aussi bien pour les adultes que pour les enfants. L'énorme lettre était autrefois un N pour Ecole Normale, puis un T pour Tempe. Aujourd'hui, le A illustre le sigle de l'université (ASU).

El Tempe Butte es una colina popular con los niños y adultos. La letra fue anteriormente una N para la Escuela Normal, y despúes una T, para el Colegio Estatal de Maestros de Tempe. Hoy día la A representa la U.E. de A.

Der Tempe Butte ist ein charakteristisches Kennzeichen und ein Spielplatz für Kinder und Erwachsene. Der riesige Buchstabe war einst ein N für Normal School, dann ein T für Tempe State Teachers College (Lehrerkolleg). Heute steht das A für Arizona State University.

テンピのビューツは特異なみどころであり、子供だけでなく大人も楽しめる遊び場でもある。巨大な字はかつてはノーマル・スクールの頭文字をとったNであったが、後にテンピ州立教員大学の頭文字をとったTに変わり、現在ではアリゾナ州立大学を表わすAの文字が描かれている。

page 37

Les nouveaux arrivants ne mettent pas longtemps à apprécier puis à soutenir leur communauté d'adoption. Ce groupe affiche les couleurs des Suns de Phoenix, une équipe qui est parvenue en finale du championnat national de basketball en 1993.

"Popladores" nuevos no tardan en disfrutar y apoyar a sus comunidad adoptiva. Este grupo muestra los colores de los Phoenix Suns, que competicieron en el campeonato de 1993 de la Associación Nacional de Básquetbol.

Neue "Siedler" brauchen nicht lange bis sie ihre neu angenommene Heimat genießen und unterstützen. Diese Gruppe präsentiert die Farben der Phoenix Suns, die 1993 um die Meisterschaft der National Basketball Association kämpften.

新しい「開拓者」達はこの地域をサポートし、エンジョイしている。このグループは全米バスケット・ボール協会の1993年度のチャンピオンシップを競い合ったフェニックス・サンズのチーム・カラーを見せている。

page 38

Chaque année, la parade du Fiesta Bowl est une occasion de faire revivre des traditions. Cette petite fille évoque l'élégance romantique du vieux Sud.

Cada año, el desfile del Fiesta Bowl ofrece la oportunidad de revivir las tradiciones. Una niña expone la elegancia romántica sureña.

Jedes Jahr bietet die Fiesta Bowl Parade eine Möglichkeit Traditionen wiederaufleben zu lassen. Ein kleines Mädchen zeigt südliche malerische Eleganz.

毎年フィエスタ．ボール・パレードでは伝統を復興させる絶好のチャンスである。少女が南部のロマンチックなエレガントさをかもしだしている。

page 39

Un jeune danseur Hopi semble absorbé dans ses souvenirs avant d'entrer dans la parade.

Un joven bailador Hopi està perdido en sus memorias.

Ein junger Hopi Tänzer ist in Gedanken versunken.

若いホピ族のインディアン・ダンサーが郷愁にひたっている

page 40

page 41

Les courses du Fiesta Bowl font partie de ces nombreuses activités qui permettent aux résidents et aux visiteurs de fraterniser.

Las carreras del Fiesta Bowl son casos que unen a la comunidad con los visitadores.

Fiesta Bowl Wettläufe sind einige von vielen Ereignissen, die die Stadtgemeinde und Besucher zusammenbringen.

フィエスタ・ボールのレースはビジ ターと地域の人々を結び付ける数多い イベントの中の一つである。

Descendre la Rivière Verte sur une bouée est une expérience qui attire beaucoup de jeunes chaque été.

La flotación en el Rio Verde es una experiencia veranal que no se la pierden los jóvenes.

Den Verde River hinunterzutreiben ist ein Sommervergnügen, auf das viele junge Leute nicht verzichten möchten.

バーデ・リバーでのチューブに乗って の川下りはヤングにとって夏を最高に 体験するアクティビティーである。

page 42

page 43

Florence Nelson a créé le Centre pour la Connaissance du Désert afin d'introduire les habitants de l'Arizona et les visiteurs aux splendeurs fragiles – flore et faune – du désert de Sonora. Le Centre, qui travaille en coordination avec divers programmes d'ASU sur l'environnement, offre aussi des présentations archéologiques sur les Hohokams, les plus anciens habitants connus de l'Arizona.

Florence Nelson fundio el Centro del Descubrimiento del Desierto para introducir los habitantes y visitadores de Arizona a los esplendores frágiles y a los moradores del desierto Sonorense. El Centro, que trabaja con otros programas de medios de ambiente de la U.E. de A., también provee presentaciones arquiológicas de los Hohokams, ancianos habitantes humanos.

Florence Nelson gründete das Desert Discovery Center um die Bewohner und Besucher von Arizona an die zerbrechliche Pracht - und die Bewohner - der Sonora Wüste heranzuführen. Das Center das mit anderen Umweltschutzprogrammen der Arizona State University zusammenarbeitet, bietet auch archäologische Darstellungen der ehemaligen menschlichen Bewohner, der Hohokams.

フローレンス・ネルソンはアリゾナの 住民とビジターにソノラン砂漠のかよ わいながらも素晴らしい自然を紹介す るためにデザート・ディスカバリー・ センターを創設した。このセンターは アリゾナ州立大学の環境プログラムと 共に運営されている。また古代の住人 であるホホカム・インディアンの考古 学の展示も提供されている。

Kay Gammage partage avec bonne humeur ses souvenirs de son mari, l'ancien président d'ASU Grady Gammage, lorsque celui-ci traitait avec Frank Lloyd Wright. Tous deux ont lancé l'idée de ce qui est aujourd'hui le Gammage Auditorium – l'une des meilleures salles de concert au monde.

Kay Gammage alegremente comparte recuerdos de su difunto esposo, y presidente de U.E. de A. Grady Gammage, que trata con Frank Lloyd Wright. Los dos iniciaron lo que ahora es el Auditorio Gammage, uno de los mejores salones de conciertos del mundo.

Fröhlich erzählt Kay Gammage von Erinnerungen an ihren verstorbenen Ehemann, den früheren ASU Präsidenten Grady Gammage, wie er mit Frank Lloyd Wright umging. Beide initiierten das, was heute das Gammage Auditorium ist, eine der besten Konzerthallen der Welt.

ケイ・ガメッジ婦人は亡くなった夫の アリゾナ州立大学の故学長であったグ ラディー・ガメッジ氏とフランク・ロ イド・ライト氏との楽しい思い出を分 かち合う。彼らは共にガメッジ大講堂 を設立し、これは現在では世界でも最 高峰のコンサート・ホールとなってい る。

page 44

page 45

Ron Gasowski, professeur d'arts appliqués à ASU et lui-même un artiste reconnu, laisse à son imagination la liberté de créer des sculptures poétiques à l'aide de débris de céramique soit trouvés soit faits spécialement.

Ron Gasowski, profesor de arte en la U.E. de A. y un artista acertado, dispara su imaginación en la creación de esculturas poéticas al usar objetos de cerámica hallados y hechos a mano.

Ron Gasowski, Kunstprofessor an der ASU, läßt seiner Phantasie freien Lauf beim Schaffen seiner Skulpturen, indem er gegossene und handgearbeitete Keramiken gebraucht.

アリゾナ州立大学の芸術学部の教授であり、また成功している芸術家でもあるロン・ガソウスキー氏は手作りのセラミックを使い、詩的な彫刻に創造力をかきたたせている。

James DeMars (à droite), professeur à l'Ecole de Musique d'ASU, s'est fait une réputation nationale pour ses compositions mêlant la flûte indienne à des instruments classiques, et pour une nouvelle oeuvre intitulée *Un Requiem Américain*. Le poète Alberto "Tito" Rios, qui dirige les programmes d'Ecriture Créative d'ASU, a lui aussi une réputation nationale.

James DeMars, profesor de música en la U.E. de A. recibe atención nacional por sus composiciones musicales que unen instrumentos clásicos y de los indios americanos, y para una nueva obra intitulada *An American Requiem*. El poeta Alberto Rios, encabezado de los programas de escritura creativa en inglés de la U.E. de A., ha recibido reconocimiento nacional por su obra.

James DeMars, Professor an der ASU-Fakultät für Musik, erregt Aufmerksamkeit in der ganzen Nation für seine Kompositionen, die klassische und indianische Instrumente zusammenfügen, und für eine neue Arbeit mit Namen *An American Requiem*. Der Dichter Alberto Tito Rios, der Vorsitzende des Englisch Creative Writing Programmes an der ASU erhielt nationale Anerkennung für seine Arbeit.

page 46

page 47

Le maire de Tempe, Harry Mitchell, apprécie visiblement la compagnie de Miss Arizona pendant le défilé du Fiesta Bowl, avec des volontaires des Tempe Diablos.

El alcalde de Tempe, Harry Mitchell goza de la companía de Miss Arizona en el desfile del Fiesta Bowl con voluntarios de los Diablos de Tempe.

Bürgermeister Harry Mitchell genießt die Gesellschaft von Miss Arizona in der Fiesta Bowl Parade, zusammen mit den eifrigen Helfern von Tempe Diablos.

フィエスタ・ボール・パレードではテンピ市長のハリー・ミッチェル氏がテンピのディアブロ・スタジアムのボランティアーを脇に、ミス・アリゾナの同伴をエンジョイしている。

Tex Earnhardt a fondé l'un des centres de distribution automobile les plus importants d'Amérique, à l'époque où Tempe était une agglomération rurale. Adepte de longue date des rodéos, il monte ici son taureau Brahma dont il a fait le symbole de sa compagnie.

Tex Earnhardt empezó uno de los más acertados negocios de coches del país cuando Tempe era todavía terreno de agrícola. Participante por mucho tiempo en los rodeos, monta aquí el toro Brahma que se ha hecho su nombre comercial.

Tex Earnhardt begann eine der erfolgreichsten Autohandelsfirmen der Nation, als Tempe noch landwirtschaftliches Gebiet war. Er ist ein langjähriger Teilnehmer an Rodeos und reitet hier den Brahma Stier, der sein Warenzeichen geworden ist.

テックス・アーンハートはテンピがまだ農業用地であった時から車のディーラーシップを始め、現在では全米で最も成功しているディーラーとなった。彼は長年にわたるロデオの参加者であり、ここで水牛に乗り、これが彼のトレードマークとなっている。

page 48

page 50

Les Cardinaux de Phoenix sont l'équipe locale, membre de la Ligue Nationale. Leurs supporters portent leurs couleurs avec fierté.

Los Cardinales de Phoenix son el equipo del Valle del Sol en la Liga Profesional de Fútbol. Sus aficionados guarden sus colores con orgullo.

Die Phoenix Cardinals sind das Profi-Football Team für das Valley of the Sun. Seine Fans zeigen stolz seine Farben.

フェニックス・カーディナルスはここ太陽の渓谷を本拠地とする全米フットボール・チームである。ファンの人達が誇りを持ってチーム・カラーを抱いている。

Art et créativité sont omniprésents dans le paysage urbain de Tempe.

El arte y la creación son ingredientes omnipresentes del paisaje urbano de Tempe.

Kunst und Kreativität sind immer gegenwärtige Zutaten im Stadtgebiet von Tempe.

芸術と創造性がテンピの景観に遍在する要素である。

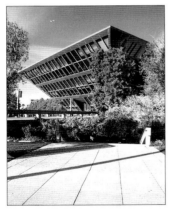

page 51

page 52

L'Hotel de Ville présente la forme d'une élégante pyramide renversée – une solution inhabituelle quoique logique aux problèmes d'économies d'énergie pour donner de l'ombre aux espaces intérieurs. Cette pyramide ne passe pas inaperçue dans le centre de Tempe.

La elegante pirámide en reversa de la Alcadía de Tempe, una rara aunque lógica solución de energía, provee espacios internos en la sombra. Es una vista característica de Tempe.

Die elegante, auf die Spitze gestellte, Pyramide von Tempe City Hall, eine ungewöhnliche und trotzdem logische und energiesparende Lösung um genügend Innenräume im Schatten zu schaffen, ist ein unverkennbarer Teil der Innenstadt von Tempe.

逆さまのピラミッドの形をしたエレガントなテンピ市役所は一般的ではないが、影を利用した論理的な省エネ対策の解決方であり、ダウンタウン・テンピの見逃せない特徴的なビルである。

Des sociétés multinationales et de grandes compagnies nationales se sont établies à Tempe en raison des avantages de la proximité de Phoenix et d'un grand aéroport, mais aussi des importants moyens de recherche disponibles à ASU et d'une qualité de vie exceptionnelle.

Las corporaciones internacionales y comercios locales son atraídos a Tempe a causa de su locación conveniente a Phoenix y a su aeropuerto, los estudios proveídos por la U.E. de A. y una vida encantadora.

Internationale Gesellschaften und wichtige regionale Firmen fühlen sich von Tempe angezogen, wegen seiner günstigen Lage in der Nähe von Phoenix und einem größeren Flughafen, durch die großen Forschungsstellen an der Arizona State University und einem verlockenden Lebensstil.

フェニックス市内および空港までの近距離な交通、またアリゾナ州立大学によって提供される大規模なリサーチ源、魅力的なライフスタイルが国際的な企業および主要なローカルの会社がテンピに魅了されている理由である。

page 53

L'usine génératrice d'Arizona Public Service apparaît comme une sorte de vaisseau spatial en arrière-plan du parcours de golf Karsten.

La planta de eléctrica que parece a une estación de espacio es un fondo de alta tecnología a la verdura atrayante del campo de golf Karsten.

Das einer Raumstation ähnelnde Kraftwerk des Arizona Public Service ist ein high-tech Hintergrund für das einladende Grün des Karsten Golfplatzes.

アリゾナ・パブリック・サービスの宇宙ステーションのような形をした発電所がカーステン・ゴルフ・コースの魅力的な緑のハイテックの背景となっている。

page 54

La société des trains Amtrak fait toujours de Tempe une croisée des chemins. Dans le fond, on peut distinguer la pyramide blanche qui est la tombe de George Hunt, le premier gouverneur d'Arizona.

Tren de Amtrak guarda la más vieja tradición de Tempe come cruce de caminos. En el fondo se ve la pirámide de la tumba de George Hunt, primer gobernador de Arizona.

Amtrak erhält Tempes älteste Tradition als Verkehrsknotenpunkt am Leben. Im Hintergrund ist das weiße, wie eine Pyramide geformte Grabmal von George Hunt, Arizonas erstem Gouverneur, sichtbar.

アムトラックが宿場町としてのテンピの古き伝統を蘇らせている。背景に見えるのはアリゾナの初代州知事ジョージ・ハントの白いプラミッドの形をした墓である。

page 55

L'aéroport de Phoenix, Shy Harbor International, est l'un des plus actifs d'Amérique. Le ciel de Tempe est le constant témoin de cette activité.

El aeropuerto internacional Sky Harbor de Phoenix es uno de los más usados del país. Visiones de aviones que aterrizan y despegan son partes de las vistas de Tempe.

Phoenix' Sky Harbor International ist einer der verkehrsreichsten Flughäfen. Der Anblick von Flugzeugen die landen und starten sind ein Teil des Himmels über Tempe.

フェニックス・スカイハーバー国際空港は最も発着の多い空港の一つで、ジョット機の往来がテンピの都市風景の一部となっている。

page 56

Lors de chaque Nouvel An, la parade du Fiesta Bowl, son concours de fanfares et son match de football captivent l'attention de tout le pays.

Cuando llega el año nuevo, el desfile del Fiesta Bowl, el concurso de bandas en marcha, y el partido de fútbol, se convierten en el centro de atención nacional.

Jedes Jahr an Silvester stehen die Fiesta Bowl Parade, der Wettbewerb der Marching Bands und das Football Spiel im Mittelpunkt des nationalen Interesses.

年末に行なわれるフィエスタ・ボール・パレードではマーチング・バンド・コンテストとフットボールのゲームが全米で注目の的となる。

page 57

Une vue aérienne révèle l'impressionnante architecture du stade des Sun Devils d'ASU, qui peut asseoir jusqu'à 75.000 spectateurs.

Una vista del Estadio Sun Devil con una capacidad de 75,000 aficionados.

Ein Luftbild zeigt die eindrucksvolle Architektur des ASU Sun Devil Stadions, das Platz für 75.000 Menschen bietet.

7万5千人を収容するアリゾナ州立大学のサン・デビル・スタジアムの印象的な建築を空から眺める。

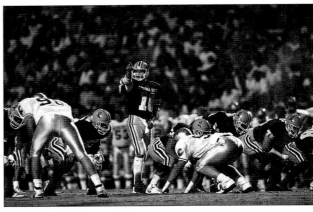

page 58

L'équipe de football d'ASU, les Sun Devils, jouent à domicile devant des foules enthousiastes.

El equipo de fútbol de la U.E. de A. juega en frente de aficionados entusiastas.

Die ASU Football Mannschaft, die Sun Devils, spielen ein Heimspiel vor einer begeisterten Menge.

アリゾナ州立大学のフットボール・チームであるサン・デビルズがホームグラウンドにおいて熱狂的な観衆の前で試合を行なう。

page 59

Le climat ensoleillé de l'Arizona attirent les équipes de baseball pour l'entraînement de printemps. Les Anges de Californie ont adopté le tout nouveau Diablo Stadium de Tempe.

El tiempo templado de Arizona favorece a los equipos de béisbol que entrenan aquí en la primavera. Los Angeles de California entrenan en el nuevo Estadio Diablo de Tempe.

Das sonnige Wetter in Arizona ist ein Segen für das Training auswärtiger Baseball Teams im Frühling. Die California Angels haben das neue Tempe Diablo Stadion übernommen.

太陽の降り注ぐアリゾナの気候は野球の春期のトレーニング・キャンプには絶好である。テンピのディアブロ・スタジアムがカリフォルニア・エンジェルスのトレーニングの新しい本拠地となった。

page 60

La petite communauté de Guadalupe, adjacente à Tempe, a été fondée au début du siècle par des indiens Yaquis qui fuyaient le Mexique. Des peintures murales affichent avec fierté son identité culturelle.

La alda pequeña de Guadalupe, establecida por los Yaquis de México al empezar del siglo, enseña orgullosamente sus murales que exponen su identidad cultural.

Die kleine benachbarte Gemeinde von Guadalupe, die von Yaqui Einwanderern aus Mexiko Anfang des Jahrhunderts gegründet wurde, zeigt stolz die Eigenheit seiner Kultur auf Wandgemälden.

今世紀の初頭にメキシコから移動したヤキ・インディアンによって設立された小さなテンピ市に隣接するコミュニティーがグアダルペである。屋外の壁に彼らの文化のアイデンティティーが誇らしげに象徴されている。

page 61

La mosquée du Centre Islamique, dans le centre de Tempe, illustre avec élégance la diversité de cultures qui donne à Tempe sa specificité.

El mezquita del Centro Islamito de Tempe demuestra con gracia la diversidad de culturas que hace especial a esta comunidad.

Die Moschee des Islamic Center im Zentrum von Tempe illustriert würdevoll die Verschiedenheit von Kulturen, die diese Stadtgemeinde so außergewöhnlich machen.

ダウンタウン・テンピにあるイスラム教のモスクがこの地域を特異なものとしており、テンピ市の文化の多様性を物語っている。

page 62-63

Entouré par des étangs et par une végétation luxuriante, le Zoo de Phoenix est le zoo non subventionné le plus important au monde. Situé en partie sur le territoire de Tempe à Papago Park, sur la rive nord de la Rivière Salée, ce zoo est un lieu de rêve pour les amoureux de la nature et des animaux.

El Zológico de Phoenix, rodeado de lagos y de vegetación espléndida es el más grande de los zológicos no apodados por impuestos. Situado en parte en Tempe, en el Parque Papago, del otro lado del Río Salado, ofrece paseos agradables a los amantes de naturaleza y animales.

Der Phoenix Zoo ist einer der größten, nicht durch Steuern subventionierten, Zoos der Welt, umgeben von kleinen Seen und einer üppigen Vegetation. Er liegt teilweise in Tempe im Papago Park, gerade gegenüber vom Salt River, und bietet wohltuende Wanderungen für Natur-und Tierliebhaber.

池と豊かな植物に覆われたフェニックス動物園は税金により運営されていない世界最大の動物園である。テンピ市内のパパゴ公園内に位置し、ソルト・リバーを脇に位置する。自然と動物愛好家にとって心地良い散歩道を提供している。

page 64

De nombreuses oeuvres d'art contemporain font du campus d'ASU une étonnante galerie d'art à ciel ouvert. *Celebration* par Jerry Peart a été commandé en 1984 pour le centenaire d'ASU.

Obras de arte contemporaneo cambia a los terrenos de la U.E. de A. en una galería de arte. La "Celebración" de Jerry Peart fue ordenada en 1984 para las festividades centinarias de la U.E. de A.

Arbeiten zeitgenössischer Kunst verwandeln den Campus der Arizona State University in eine interessante Freiluftkunstgallerie. Jerry Parts *Celebration* wurde im Jahr 1984 für die Jahrhundertfeier der ASU in Auftrag gegeben.

現代芸術の作品がアリゾナ州立大学のキャンパスを興味深い屋外の芸術ギャラリーへと変換している。ジェリー・ピアーツの作品「セレブレーション」は1984年に開催されたアリゾナ州立大学の創立百周年の記念祭で制作が依頼された。

page 66

page 67

Armstrong Hall, qui fait partie de l'Ecole de Droit d'ASU, porte le nom du jeune Député Territorial qui a fondé en 1885 l'Ecole Normale de Tempe – laquelle devait plus tard devenir l'Université d'Etat d'Arizona. Aujourd'hui, le campus a aussi vocation de jardin botanique, où sont conservées une grande variété de plantes du désert et de végétaux rares.

Armstrong Hall, escuela de leyes de la U.E. de A. fue nombrada por el joven legislador territorial que fundó en 1885 la Escuela Normal de Tempe. Se transformó más tarde en la U.E. de A. Hoy los terrenos sirven también como un jardín botánico que proveen con una variedad de toda clase de flora del desierto y de raras vegetales.

Die Armstrong Hall der Rechts-fakultät der ASU wurde benannt nach dem jungen Gesetzgeber des Territoriums der im Jahr 1885 die Tempe Normal School gründete, die später die Arizona State University wurde. Heute dient der Campus auch als ein Arboretum das eine Vielzahl von wüstenspezifischen und seltenen Pflanzenarten zeigt.

アリゾナ州立大学法律学部のアームストロング・ホールは1885年にテンピ・ノーマル・スクールを設立した若い準州時代の議員にちなんで名付けられた。この学校は後にアリゾナ州立大学となった。

Lieu de passage très fréquenté, Palm Walk traverse le campus du nord au sud. D'immenses palmiers y projettent leur ombre caracté-ristique.

Un paseo popular, el Palm Walk cruza los terrenos del norte y al sur, bajo la sombra distinguida de palmeras altas.

Der Palm Walk, ein beliebter Weg über den Campus, durchquert den Campus von Norden nach Süden, unter dem unverkennbaren Schatten von turmhohen Palmen.

キャンパスの南北を走るポピュラーな歩道、パーム・ウォークは聳え立つパームトゥリーが独特な影を創っている。

page 68

page 69

La croissance rapide d'ASU ces vingt dernières années a nourri le besoin pour de nouveaux équipements. Sous l'égide du Collège d'Architecture et d'Etudes d'Environnement, de superbes bâtiments ont été construits qui attirent sur le campus d'ASU des architectes du monde entier.

El rápido crecimiento de la U.E. de A. en las dos últimas décadas ha exigido una necesidad por facilidades nuevas. Bajo la supervisión del Colegio de Arquitectura y Diseño de Inme-diaciones edificios sobresalientes han sido construídos que hacen de la U.E. de A. una atracción en sí misma por arquitectos.

Das ungestüme Wachstum der ASU in den letzten beiden Jahrzehnten hat einen Bedarf für neue Gebäude hervorgerufen. Unter der Aufsicht des College of Architecture and Environmental Design wurden hervorragende Gebäude errichtet, die den Campus der ASU selbst zu einer Sehenswürdigkeit für Architekten macht.

過去20年間にわたるアリゾナ州立大学の驚異的な成長は新しい施設の建設を余儀なくした。建築・環境デザイン学部の指導の下にアリゾナ州立大学のキャンパスの建築設計がなされ、素晴らしいビル群それ自体が魅力的なキャンパスを創っている。

Un groupe d'étudiants apprécient le soleil matinal dans la fraîcheur d'un jour de printemps, autour de la fontaine qui fait face au nouveau bâtiment des Sciences de la Vie. Dans le fond se devine Old Main (la "Grande Vieille"), le premier bâtiment construit sur le campus, en 1898.

Unos estudiantes gozan del sol matinal de un fresco día de primavera al lado de la fuente situada en frente del nuevo edificio de Ciencias de Vida. En el fondo se ve Old Main (Viejo Grande), el primer edificio de la universidad, construído en 1898.

Am Brunnen, der vor dem neuen Life Sciences Gebäude steht, genießt eine Gruppe von Studenten die Morgensonne an einem kühlen Frühlingsmorgen. Im Hintergrund steht Old Main, das erste Gebäude auf dem Campus, erbaut im Jahr 1898.

生徒達が新しい生命科学の校舎の前に位置する泉の脇で心地よい朝の太陽の光をエンジョイしている。背景はオールド・メインと呼ばれる建造物で、1898年にこのキャンパスで最初に建築された。

page 70

L'architecture du nouveau bâtiment des Services Etudiants offre de spectaculaires perspectives.

La arquitectura del nuevo edificio para Servicios Estudiantiles dispone perspectivas espectulares.

Die Architektur des neuen Student Services Gebäudes bietet eindrucksvolle Perspektiven.

新しいスチューデント・サービス・ビルの建築からは豪快な眺めが見られる。

page 71

Cette chambre acoustique spécialement construite pour un projet illustre l'engagement d'ASU dans les recherches les plus avancées.

Esta cámara de acústicos demuestra la dedicación de la U.E. de A. a los estudios científicos.

Diese speziell gebaute Akustikkammer kennzeichnet die Verpflichtung der ASU zu äußerst fortschrittlicher wissenschaftlicher Forschung.

この特別に作られた音響部屋は先端を行くアリゾナ州立大学の科学リサーチに対する熱意を象徴している。

page 72

Le Nelson Arts Center a été conçu par le célèbre architecte Antoine Predock. Il abrite les collections d'art d'ASU et offre d'inventifs espaces de spectacles, à la fois intérieurs et extérieurs.

El Centro de Artes Nelson fue deseñado por el celebre arquitecto Antoine Predock. Abriga colecciones de arte y ofrece espacios para espectaculos y presentaciones interiores y exteriores.

Das Nelson Kunstzentrum wurde entworfen von dem bekannten Architekten Antoine Predock. Es beherbergt die Kunstsammlungen der ASU und bietet außergewöhnliche Räume für darstellende Kunst in Innenräumen und im Freien.

ネルソン・アート・センターは著名な建築家アントイン・プレドックにより設計された。ここではアリゾナ州立大学の芸術コレクションおよび奇抜な屋外・屋内の演奏演劇の場を提供している。

page 73

Les fontaines forment un thème sur le campus d'ASU. Les étudiants en font bon usage pendant les chaudes journées d'été.

Las fuentes son siempre presentes en la U.E. de A. Son bienvenidas para los estudiantes durante los días cálidos de verano.

Wasserspiele sind überall auf dem Campus zu finden. Sie werden an den heißen Sommertagen von den Studenten besonders begrüßt.

アリゾナ州立大学のキャンパスは水を特徴としたデザインが至る所に見られる。夏の暑い期間は生徒達にとっては大歓迎である。

page 74

page 75

Chaque année apporte d'intéressantes additions au paysage du campus. Avec ses formes résolument futuristes, la nouvelle Bibliothèque de Droit perpétue cette tradition d'innovation.

Cada año trae una nueva vista a los terrenos. Con sus formas futurísticas la nueva Biblioteca de Leyes acentúa otra innovación.

Jedes Jahr bringt einen neuen Zuwachs für die Skyline der ASU. Mit seinen futuristischen Formen, führt die neue Rechtsbibliothek die Tradition kühner Innovationen fort.

毎年キャンパスには新たな豪快な建物が追加される。未来を現わすような奇抜な形をした新しい法律図書館のデザインはその大胆さを将来に永続させるだろう。

ASU est la 5ème université d'Amérique par le nombre d'étudiants. Allées et bâtiments sont sans cesse parcourus par une foule pressée.

La Universidad Estatal de Arizona es ahora la quinta más grande de los Estados Unidos. Paseos y edificios están llenos de estudiantes en prisa.

Die Arizona State University ist jetzt die fünftgrößte Universität in den Vereinigten Staaten. Wege und Gebäude auf dem Campus sind bevölkert von geschäftigen Menschenmengen.

アリゾナ州立大学は現在全米で5番目の規模を誇る大学である。キャンパスの歩道と校舎は小走りに急ぐ生徒達であふれている。

page 76

page 77

Illustration de la vie universitaire, les panneaux d'affichage témoignent de l'imagination étudiante.

Una reflección de la vida estudiantil, anuncios muestran la imaginación de los estudiantes.

Anzeigentafeln stellen phantasievolle Ankündigungen zur Schau, als ein Spiegelbild des Campuslebens.

キャンパス・ライフを反映する掲示板のディスプレーに生徒の想像的なニュースが載っている。

Le campus d'ASU, avec plus de 45.000 étudiants, est une ville en soi. La nouvelle aile du Collège d'Architecture et d'Etudes d'Environnement contribue à nourrir cette impression.

La ciudad universitaria, con sus 45.000 estudiantes, es en si misma un pequeño pueblo. La nueva parte del Colegio de Arquitectura y Diseño de Inmediaciones contribúe a este sentimiento.

Der ASU Campus, der 45.000 Studenten beherbergt, ist eine kleine Stadt in sich. Der neue Flügel des College of Architecture and Environmental Design trägt zu diesem Stadtgefühl bei.

45,000人以上の生徒を収容するアリゾナ州立大学はそれ自体で小さな町ほどの様相をなしている。建築・環境デザイン学部の新校舎が都会的なフィーリングを引き立てている。

page 78

page 79

La cérémonie de remise des diplômes, qui se tient ici au Centre d'Activités d'ASU, perpétue dans un cérémonial haut en couleurs la tradition séculaire qui veut que soit honoré l'effort d'acquisition du savoir.

La ceremonia de graduación, aquí en el Centro de Actividades, perpetúa a colores la antigua tradición de honrar el esfuerzo de educarse.

Die Zeremonie der Entlaßfeier, die hier im ASU Activity Center abgehalten wird, setzt mit großem Erfolg die jahrhundertealte Tradition fort, das Bestreben zur Aneignung von Wissen zu ehren.

ここアリゾナ州立大学アクティビティー・センターで行なわれるカラフルな卒業式は知識を得るために努力した人々に栄誉を報ずるための儀式であり百年の伝統を有する。

Le Gammage Auditorium fournit un cadre unique aux professeurs en grand uniforme, un jour de remise des diplômes.

El Auditorio Grady Gammage provee una vista espectacular al profesorado en toda su gloria el día de graduación.

Am Tag der Entlaßfeier bietet das Grady Gammage Auditorium einen spektakulären Hintergrund für die Fakulätsmitglieder der ASU in vollem Ornat.

グラディー・ガメッジ大講堂は卒業式の日に標章においてアリゾナ州立大学教授陣に壮大な背景を提供する。

page 80

page 82

Depuis les canaux d'irrigation creusés voici des siècles jusqu'aux innombrables fontaines contemporaines, le thème d'une eau courante et bouillonnante se retrouve partout à Tempe.

Desde viejos canales para regar hasta las muchas fuentes, el tema de aguas corriendo se ven por todo Tempe.

Von jahrhundertealten Bewässerungskanälen bis zu unzähligen zeitgenössischen Brunnen, das Thema von laufendem und blubberndem Wasser ist in Tempe jederzeit gegenwärtig.

何百年もの歴史を有する灌漑用運河から現代的な噴水に至るまで、流れ泡立つ水の流れはテンピ市内の各所で見受けられる。

La rencontre miraculeuse d'un ciel toujours bleu, d'une eau abondante et d'un sol fertile a pour résultat des ensembles résidentiels qui rssemblent à des jardins.

El miraculoso encuentro del cielo siempre azul, agua en abundencia, y terreno fértil nos da vecindades residenciales bellos como jardines.

Das wunderbare Zusammentreffen eines ständig blauen Himmels, Wasser in Hülle und Fülle und fruchtbarer Erde ergibt die gartengleichen Wohngebiete in Tempe.

真青な空、豊かな水源、肥えた土地、これら要素の奇跡的とも言える遭遇により庭園の様な近隣住宅街を創っている。

page 83

Tempe comporte de nombreux lacs pour le plus grand bonheur de ses résidents.

Tempe tiene muchos lagos de los cuales sus habitantes pueden gozar.

Tempe bietet viele Seen zum Vergnügen der Bewohner.

テンピ市は市民がエンジョイ出来るように多くの湖をアメニティーとしている。

page 84

PointCentral sur Mill Avenue est le lieu de rendez-vous favori des étudiants, des professeurs et des touristes. La Butte de Tempe s'aperçoit en arrière-plan.

Punta del Centro, en la Avenida Mill, es un lugar favorito de los alumnos, profesores y de visitadores. La colina Tempe se ve al fondo.

Der Center Point auf der Mill Avenue ist ein Treffpunkt, sowohl für ASU Studenten und Fakultätsmitglieder, als auch für Besucher. Im Hintergrund ist der Tempe Butte sichtbar.

ミル・アベニューにあるセンター・ポイントはアリゾナ州立大学の生徒、先生、ビジターの間で大人気の溜まり場である。テンピのビューツが背景に見える。

page 85

Le centre de Tempe a été entièrement réhabilité ces dix dernières années. Hayden Square est une combinaison réussie de séduisantes résidences urbaines, bureaux, boutiques, restaurants et spectacles. Les Tempéens l'ont adopté.

El centro de Tempe fue renovado completamente en la última década. La PLaza Hayden combina viviendas urbanas con oficinas, tiendas, restaurantes y diversión – al encanto de los Tempineños.

Das Zentrum von Tempe wurde in den letzten zehn Jahren vollständig aufgefrischt. Der Hayden Square kombiniert attraktives städtisches Wohnen mit Büros, Geschäften, Restaurants und Unterhaltung. Die Bewohner von Tempe sind begeistert.

ダウンタウン・テンピはここ10年間で完全に復興された。ヘイデン・スクウェアーは都会的なマンション、オフィス、店舗、レストラン、エンターテイメントの魅力的な集合体である。テンピの市民の最も人気のあるスポットである。

page 86

Deux fois par an, le Festival des Arts de Tempe, le plus important de ce genre en Arizona, attire des centaines d'artistes et des foules curieuses.

Dos veces al año, el Festival de Artes de Tempe, el más grande de Arizona, reune a cienes de artistas y a muchedumbres interesadas.

Zweimal im Jahr bringt der Tempe Arts Festival, der größte seiner Art in Arizona, Hunderte von Künstlern und eine begeisterte Menge zusammen.

テンピ・アート・フェスティバルはこの種類のフェスティバルに関してはアリゾナ州では最大規模で、2年に1度開催されている。何百人もの芸術家達を集め沢山の興味を抱いた人々が集って来る。

page 87

Un peintre-sur-visage montre son talent à l'occasion du Festival des Arts.

Una pintadora de caras nos muestra su talento durante el Festival de Artes.

Eine Künstlerin, die Gesichter bemalt, zeigt ihre Kunst während des Kunstfestivals.

フェース・ペイントのアーティストが アート・フェスティバルで彼女の才能 をみせている。

page 88

Ces dernières années, Tempe est devenu un important centre d'affaires. De superbes ensembles de bureaux ont partout surgi du sol.

En los años recientes, Tempe se ha convertido en un centro de comercio. Se ven por todos lados espacios de trabajo.

In den letzten Jahren hat sich Tempe zu einem wesentlichen Geschäfts-zentrum entwickelt. Attraktive Arbeitsplätze schossen überall in der Stadt wie Pilze hervor.

近年、テンピは主要なビジネスの中心 地となってきている。魅力的な職場が 町全体で著しい成長をとげている

page 89

Apport dominant dans la restauration du centre de Tempe, l'immeuble de la Chase est au centre d'un complexe qui comprend le plus important groupe de cinémas de toute la Vallée.

Una alta adición del centro de Tempe, el edificio Chase es un lugar de muchos usos que incluye el grupo de cines más grande de todo el Valle.

Eine herausragende Beigabe zur Erneuerung der Innenstadt von Tempe ist das Chase-Gebäude, das Zentrum eines Vielzweck-Projektes, das ebenso den größten Kino-komplex des Tales einschließt.

ダウンタウン・テンピの改修には聳え 立つチエイス銀行のビルが追加され、 この建物はフェニックス大都市圏で最 大規模の映画館を含む多目的利用プロ ジェクトのセンターである。

page 90

Tempe offre des équipements de grande qualité qui contribuent à attirer conventions et touristes dans la région.

Tempe contribúe facilidades de primera clase a la atracción de convenciones y de turistas a la región.

Tempe bietet erstklassige Gegebenheiten um Tagungen und Touristen für diese Gegend zu gewinnen.

テンピ市はコンベンションおよび観光 産業に関してこの地域で第一級の施設 を提供している。

page 91

Avec plus de 50 parcours de golf, la Vallée du Soleil s'est acquis la réputation de paradis des golfeurs. Les buttes de Tempe forment l'arrière-plan du terrain d'entraînement de Fiesta Inn.

Con más de 50 campos de golf, el Valle del Sol se ha hecha muy popular con sus jugadores. He aquí el campo de ensayo del Fiesta Inn, con las colinas en el fondo.

Mit mehr als 50 Turniergolfplätzen, hat sich das Valley of the Sun als Paradies für Golfer einen Namen gemacht. Hier ist der Übungsplatz bei der Fiesta Inn, mit den Buttes im Hintergrund.

50以上のトーナメント級のゴルフコースを有する、ここ太陽の渓谷はゴルファーの天国としてその名を確固たるものとしている。これはビューツを背景に、フィエスタ・インのドライビング・レンジである。

page 92

Le Vieux Tempe révèle de nouvelles amusantes surprises chaque jour. Les boutiques de Mill's Court ont toujours un grand succès.

El Viejo Tempe provee sorpresas divertidas día tras día. Las tiendas del Mill's Court siempre son favoritas.

Das Old Tempe bietet Tag für Tag unterhaltsame Überraschungen. Die Läden am Mill's Court sind ein ständiger Favorit.

オールド・テンピでは毎日のように楽しい驚きが人々を楽しませている。ミルズ・コートにあるこれらのお店は市民のお気に入りである。

page 93

Mill Avenue associe la simplicité d'une bourgade du Far-West avec la sophistication d'une ville universitaire.

La Avenida Mill combina el encanto de un pueblo de frontera con la sofisticación que viene de la presencia de una universidad grande.

Die Mill Avenue kombiniert den Charme einer westlichen Pionierstadt mit der Kultiviertheit, die in der Gegenwart einer großen Universität entsteht.

ミル・アベニューは大規模な大学の存在により生まれた知的さと開拓者の街のチャーミングな味わいが重なり合った通りである。

page 94

A Kiwanis Park, la nouvelle génération montre le chemin de l'avenir avec une détermination gracieuse.

En el Parque Kiwanis, la generación joven se dirige al futuro con una determinación graciosa.

Im Kiwanis Park zeigt die junge Generation den Weg in die Zukunft mit anmutiger Entschlossenheit.

キワニス公園では若い世代が未来を指差し、決意を固めている。

page 95

page 96

La fleur du cactus dit Prickly Pear (littéralement, "la poire qui pique") symbolise ici l'émergence de Tempe hors des paysages rugueux du désert de Sonora.

La flor del nopal simboliza aquí la emergencia de Tempe del brusco desierto sonorense.

Die Blüte des Prickly Pear Kaktusses symbolisiert das Blühen Tempes in der Wüste Sonora.

プリックリー・ペア・サボテンの花は ソノラン砂漠の荒野の砂漠から開花し たテンピを象徴している。

Cette vue de Tempe illustre la vision de Charles Trumbull Hayden: une cité active et prospère sur la rive sud de la Rivière Salée.

Esta vista de Tempe ilustra la visión de Charles Trumbull Hayden de una comunidad viva y próspera a la orilla sur del Río Salado.

Dieser Blick auf Tempe veranschaulicht Charles Trumbull Haydens Vision einer pulsierenden und blühenden Stadtgemeinde am Südufer des Salt River.

ソルト・リバーの南側に存在する活力 ある繁栄の街、これがチャールズ・ト ランブル・ヘイデンがテンピに対して 描いたビジョンである。

Note of the author.

My photographs appearing in this book were taken specifically for this purpose, from June, 1992, through July, 1993. All are original material.

I express my gratitude to the residents of Tempe who provided me with advice and introductions, welcomed me on their property or accepted to appear in this book.

My equipment included four Nikon cameras and a variety of Nikkor and Sigma lenses. The films I used were Kodachrome 64 and Kodachrome 200 exclusively.

Michel F. Sarda

Index of names

Bibliography

Archives

Arizona Historical Foundation Collection,
    Arizona State University, Tempe.

Arizona Historical Society, Tucson and Phoenix archives.

Arizona State University Library, Tempe.

Tempe Daily News (files in Tempe Historical Museum)

Tempe Town Councils. *Minutes, 1894-1920.*
    Tempe Historical Museum.

Tempe Historical Museum; transcriptions of oral history, newspaper clipping files, photography files, early Tempe families files.

Tempe Public Library.

Publications

Armstrong, Blair Morton. *Arizona Anthem.*
    Scottsdale: The Mnemosyne Press, 1982.

Fireman, Bert M. *Charles Trumbull Hayden.*
    The Smoke Signal, Nº 19 (Spring, 1969)

Haigler, Ruby. *The History of Tempe.*
    Unpublished ms. 1914. Tempe Historical Museum.

Hayden, Carl Trumbull. *Charles Trumbull Hayden, Pioneer.*
    Tucson: Arizona Historical Society, 1972.

Johnson, G. Wesley Jr. *Phoenix, Valley of the Sun.*
    Tulsa: Continental Heritage Press, 1982.

Lamb, Blaine P. *Historical Overview of Tempe, Arizona.*
    Unpublished ms. 1981. Tempe Historical Museum.

Luckingham, Bradford. *Phoenix.*
    Tucson: The University of Arizona Press, 1989.

Myers, John M. *Tempe's Story.*
    Tempe Historical Museum, 1971.

Powell, Lawrence Clark. *Arizona – A History.*
    Albuquerque: University of New Mexico Press, 1990.

Robinson, Dorothy. *A History of Early Tempe.*
    Tempe Historical Museum, c. 1959.

Schisler, Augusta. *Tempe Tales.*
    Tempe Historical Museum, 1971.

Smith, Dean. *Tempe, Arizona Crossroads.*
    Chatsworth, CA: Windsor Publications, Inc., 1990.

Solliday, Scott. *The Journey to Rio Salado:
    Hispanic Migrations to Tempe, Arizona.*
    Master's Thesis, Arizona State University, 1993.

Trimble, Marshall. *Arizona: A Cavalcade of History.*
    Tucson: Treasure Chest Publications, 1989.

Weisiger, Marsha L. *This History of Tempe, Arizona.*
    Tempe Historical Museum, 1978.

Windes, William H. *Growing Up in Tempe, 1909-1929.*
    Bound typescript, 1983. Tempe Historical Museum.

Wood, Ruby Haigler. *History of Tempe.*
    Tempe Historical Museum, 1974.

Photographers

Ken Akers
A graduate of Arizona State University, Ken joined the Tempe Daily News in 1972. After working in Alaska for a time, he worked with the *Arizona Republic* newspaper from 1980 to 1986, during which he was twice elected News Photographer of the Year. In 1988, he was designated as the Team Photographer of the Phoenix Cardinals. He now works as a free-lance photographer.

Ben Arnold
Ben covers regularly the various events of the Fiesta Bowl.

Alan Benoit
A Tempe, Arizona based photographer, Alan has published work in over 11 countries and 200 books and periodicals. Major corporations located in Arizona and throughout the United States have utilized his work to illustrate their interests in various regions. A strong love for the outdoors and natural subjects, combined with an intense curiosity for the way the people of the world live, work and play have led Alan's work to be displayed in places as diverse as the Nikon House Gallery in New York and the Sonoran Desert Museum in Tucson.

Jeff Kida
Jeff started taking photos as a hobby while attending high school in South America, and continued at Arizona State University studying political science and photojournalism. He received an internship at *Arizona Highways* magazine in 1977 and has been doing assignment work for them since. He also freelances for local and regional accounts, including Fiesta Bowl.

Jim Richardson
Based in Colorado, Jim spent some time in Tempe to make a photography book on Arizona State University.

Michel F. Sarda
A graduate architect of the Ecole Superieure des Beaux-Arts of Paris, Michel practiced photography along with architecture for more than 20 years. He wrote and contributed his photographic work to two other publications on the Valley of the Sun, *Phoenix – from legend to reality* and *Scottsdale – a portrait in color*. Also a writer and a designer, he specializes in people and architecture photography.